Did I Really Change My Underwear Every Day?

DID I REALLY CHANGE MY UNDERWEAR EVERY DAY?

One Geezer's Handbook
For (Temporary) Survival

Larry McCoy

SUNSTONE
PRESS

SANTA FE

Sunstone books may be purchased for educational, business, or sales promotional use.
For information please write: Special Markets Department, Sunstone Press,
P.O. Box 2321, Santa Fe, New Mexico 87504-2321.

Book and Cover design • Vicki Ahl
Body typeface • Humanst521 BT and Snap ITC
Printed on acid free paper

Library of Congress Cataloging-in-Publication Data

McCoy, Larry.
 Did I really change my underwear every day? : one geezer's handbook for
(temporary) survival / by Larry McCoy.
   p. cm.
 ISBN 978-0-86534-778-6 (softcover : alk. paper)
 1. Aging--Humor. I. Title.
 PN6231.A43M33 2011
 818'.602--dc23
                                        2011018095

Published in
Santa Fe

WWW.SUNSTONEPRESS.COM
SUNSTONE PRESS / POST OFFICE BOX 2321 / SANTA FE, NM 87504-2321 /USA
(505) 988-4418 / ORDERS ONLY (800) 243-5644 / FAX (505) 988-1025

With love for The Players, especially Irene,
who never gave up on me.

CONTENTS

The Players

Wife—Irene
"The Kids"—Julie and Jack.
Their spouses—Lynn and Deena.
The grandkids—Nicholas and Rachel,
the older ones from Julie and Lynn;
and Daniella and Cristiana,
the younger ones from Jack and Deena.

Prologue

One December as my wife and I approached our first Christmas as retirees, I wrote a letter to friends about the zillion questions that had popped up since we left the work force:

> Did I really use to change my underwear every day? Why?
> Did the both of us always chew that loudly at breakfast?
> Why is everyone driving so fast and so close behind us?
> How is it possible, that one errand can eat up the entire morning or afternoon?
> Why do our kids laugh, roll their eyes and look into the distance when we tell them we found this terrific place for lunch and went there three days in a row? What's funny or odd about that?
> Has *The New York Times* always had a page devoted entirely to weather? If so, how come I never spent 20 minutes every morning staring at it?
> Did all those people coming home at night on the Long Island Rail Road look that zonked when I was one of them?
> The days are shorter now than when we were working, right?

That last question echoes the cliché about retirees asking, "How did we ever have time for work?" Irene and I both worked until we were 68—she was a writer and publicist in publishing and I was a journalist—and we're still busy as hell.

Neither of us misses what publishing and journalism have become. I'm living, having fun, struggling several hours a day to cram words into coherent sentences, reading (I must confess) an enormous amount of absolute garbage on the Internet, hoping I won't die before I'm able to understand at least one poem published in *The New Yorker*, hanging out with the grandkids, pushing myself to do exercises every morning even when I don't feel like it, and shooting hoops, if a knee or something else isn't hurting. And, of course, going out for lunch, something I knew almost nothing about when I had a job.

We have been very lucky and we know it. We are both in good health, have enough income to take a few trips every year, and the people we love the most—our two kids and four grandkids—live minutes away, making it easy for us whenever we feel a need for a good hug.

Five years into retirement I could write that letter again but would add at least two other questions:

Why can't I get comfortable in bed these days?

What's happened to my arms and elbows? I don't know what to do with them. They're always in the way when I try to sleep. This wasn't a problem when I was working. What's going on?

I trust that the arms-elbow enigma and many of the other things I've encountered on the way to my 70s are common to men my age. It's good to share experiences, good to make fun of things we can't do much about.

But, believe it or not, there is some good news ahead.

Who The Hell Is That In The Mirror?

If you're a guy, one of these days you will look in the mirror and start shaking your head and screaming, "Oh, no!" Take it from me, many men our age experience this and all of us feel like shit for at least a month. Why? Because when you looked into the mirror you saw Christopher Dodd or Bill Bradley. Fine gents both but . . .

Congratulations! You are officially a member of the Turkey Neck Club of America. That means you got a wattle. Don't be confused. You've had a waddle for some time. This is different. This is a wattle. It's one of many, many ugly parts on a turkey. This one, a lump of gristle, hangs down from the neck. My dictionary says turkeys and chickens have wattles as do—lizards. Would you feel better if we called you old lizard neck? I didn't think so.

Since there's not much you can do about it, don't worry about it. As a man of leisure with lots and lots of free time, do you really want to spend it looking at yourself? Of course not. But for the sadists among you, the ones who simply can't stop looking at themselves, here are some other things most men your age have or are about to have.

Tits, as I trust you know, are always a good place to start. You've got'em, Big Guy. You may not have noticed them yet because you always shave with a T-shirt or under-shirt on. Next time you shave, do it bare-chested, then lean over the sink and look up at the mirror. See 'em? Yes, they're disgusting. Remember when you thought the day would never come when you got tired of looking at tits—in magazines, on videos or every once in a while, lucky you, live and on another person. Well, one little peek at yourself in the mirror proves that day has come. A friend of mine, a man who has developed tits, says of a particular shoe outlet, "Every time I walk by a DSW store I feel like going in and buying a pair of pumps."

Something else you probably know little about is the back of your head. It's not a place that's easy to see, so you're under the illusion there's a lot of hair back there. That isn't the case at all for many of us. It's either baby-assed bald or populated only by a few strands of vermicelli. So be it. Only a certified goofball would fool around with a comb for longer than three-tenths of a second trying to make something out of nothing. It doesn't look like Ted Koppel back there. Never did, never will. Don't do a comb over. Get over it!

While you may be disappointed in the hair on that part of your head, things are booming elsewhere. Your eyebrows grow about an inch a day and are as thick as the bristles in a horse brush. There's a hair jungle jutting out of both ears, which you try to thin out when shaving. It also seems you have to trim your nose hairs once an hour. Those babies come in both white and black these days—all part of nature's wonderful plan for you and your body.

You also, more than likely, have a belly. Your wife, when asked by you, may say you don't, but this is the same woman who says she "can't see anything with these new glasses," is on medication and just the other day called you "Spencer," which isn't your first or last name or the name of anyone you've ever known. Welcome to Bellytown. In the winter you can wear a thick sweater to help hide the belly the Mrs. denies seeing, and in the summer you will decide you look so much better with a loose shirt hanging outside your pants.

A week ago you looked at your hands and couldn't remember having that many brown spots. (If you don't remember having that many fingers, that means something else.) Brown spots are good. They signify experience. Grandkids love to look at them and ask what they are, how you got them, and if they hurt. It gets a conversation going with them, gives you a chance to dig out some of your old stories that, after hearing for the four millionth time, a certain unnamed someone has asked you to please not tell again. Not that I wish you any past pain or future misfortune, but count your blessings if you have one really good crooked finger or maybe even a stub. It fascinates the hell out of the grandkids, the ones under five anyway, and they never get tired of hearing you blow off about it. There's nothing wrong with changing the tale every time you relate it to a different little pup on your knee. What's the harm? It's only a story. You've told it so often even you don't know if it's true anymore.

The Good News: *How you look isn't nearly as important as you once thought it was.*

" . . . Vigorous Well Past His Prime."

After the death of Señor Wences, a ventriloquist known to American TV audiences from appearances on the Ed Sullivan Show, *The New York Times* said, "he remained vigorous well past his prime." Oh, really? Since Señor Wences lived to be 103, when exactly did his "prime" end? Who's in charge of determining this sort of "prime?" A select committee at the Federal Reserve? Or some politically-connected bubble head at the U.S. Department of Agriculture who four months ago worked at an Applebee's owned by his uncle?

Kiss my ass, *New York Times*. What is it those of us pigeonholed as "well past" our primes are supposed to do? Lie down next to the curb and wait for a garbage truck to come by and pick us up? Join some damn club that does some damn thing we've never done before in our lives? Pull down all the shades in the house, turn out all the lights but one and sit around in a cardigan, corduroys and cordovan wingtips with a copy of *Great Expectations* in our hands and *Wuthering Heights* playing on the TV?

Yes, for sure many of us won't match Señor Wences' longevity, but as long as we're around no one should be surprised by our energy, curiosity and intense desire to do our best at whatever we try. What's the big deal if we aren't quite as tall as we used to be? Can't stand as straight as we once did? Have brown spots all over the back of aging hands? None of that means we can't grip a tennis racket, a golf club, a kayak paddle or a basketball. A finger or two bent from arthritis doesn't stop us from competing nor diminish the urge or urgency to WIN. White hair doesn't rule out riding a bicycle around the neighborhood with both hands off the handlebars like we did at 15, keeping up with a crowd entering or leaving Yankee Stadium, writing a decent novel or a well-argued analysis of a news story, or even acting like a very spoiled young jerk at times at Dunkin' Donuts, the movies or a restaurant.

Just because you've hit 70 or some other silly number doesn't mean you've hit the wall. That it's all over. It ain't. True, a lot of your life is behind you, but there's still more ahead to be experienced and enjoyed. Pay attention and you might even be able to remember part of it.

The Good News: *The way the news business is going there may not be any reporters around when you die to judge how well you did before, during, or past your "prime."*

An Abridged History Of Squirrels

You don't hear as well as you used to. This has been coming on for years, and your wife/companion has been kind enough to remind you of it from time to time. She fumes that "you're deaf" after repeating something a couple of times. One way to handle this cockiness is to look right at her, move your lips and gesture grandly, but not say a word. Occasionally you'll get her to bite and she'll ask, "What?"

Even before you began to lose a little range—the high notes are said to go first in aging males—there were still times of total miscommunication. After I got up from a nap one summer Saturday, Irene was outside doing yard work with a radio tuned to the Yankee game, loud enough, I might add, for all of Long Island as well as all ships at sea to hear. I asked, through the raised kitchen window, "What's the score?"

"Squirrels," she said.

I tried again, this time a little louder. "What's the SCORE?"

Same response but louder. "SQUIRRELS."

Maybe there is a professional baseball team somewhere called the Squirrels. "Now batting for the San Antonio Squirrels—Bobby Robertson." Maybe. But the Yankees are a classy bunch, and they sure as hell wouldn't play any team called the Squirrels.

Since this was getting me nowhere, I listened long enough to the play-by-play to hear that it was 6-3, Yankees over the Red Sox. Although the Red Sox and their fans may be weasels—in the eyes of this Yankees fan—I would never call them squirrels. Since Irene was standing near one of her flower beds, I assume what she was trying to relay to me was the damage done by squirrels.

While there have been studies of the loss of hearing among men my age, has there been any research into the tendency of older women to mumble? Huh? Has there? When Irene was still working and I wasn't, she came home one evening and talked about a woman in her office. I swear she said the woman was a "bending machine," a description, which frankly was quite appealing to someone who had been cooped up in the house all day by himself with no access to dirty magazines or Taxi Cab Confessions on cable TV.

This was around the same time that I was sure an announcer at an all-news radio station had read a news item that had something to do with "team pregnancy." My immediate reaction was, I wonder how that happened? That was followed by: Do insurance companies pay for these sorts of things? Do babies born as a result of a "team pregnancy" get a lot of extra names, say something like Thomas Michael Dudley Jeff Nigel Charles William? And how is the last name decided on?

Things on the hearing front aren't helped if you have a grandchild 14 or thereabouts and female. These young ladies not only have the fastest text messaging thumbs in the business theyalsotalkrealfast. There have been times when Rachel, our smart, funny, oldest granddaughter, would say something so rapidly that, not only couldn't I make out a word of it, I wasn't even sure she was speaking English. It all went by my ears faster than a blur. Maybe we could call it a flur.

Julie and Lynn, her parents, say they can understand her, most of the time, but I've been at dinner with them when they both would shake their heads and ask, "What?" My own feeling is this is a phase teenage girls go through, sort of a dress rehearsal for the mumbling technique they will perfect when they get to be Grandma's age.

The Good News: *If your hearing isn't perfect, don't worry about it. Most of what any of us say—young or old—isn't really worth repeating.*

Where Do I Get My Black Socks?

When you were a kid, I'll bet you assumed that old people had all the answers. I know I did. As I approached 70, I realized I didn't know squat. Some examples.

Why has the U.S. Congress never passed a law making it illegal for parents to lie to their children about chicken? Why have millions of us, subjected to this preposterous deception when we were young, merely shrugged and done nothing to stop it when we became adults? Not all that long ago a chunk of pork ("the other white meat") was cut up and put on the plate of Daniella, my middle granddaughter, and both Mommy and Daddy urged her to "eat your chicken." To no one's surprise, she didn't, and as the "eat your chicken" plea was repeated over and over I wanted to yell, "Give her some damn chicken and maybe she will."

That's not the only thing I don't understand. Who's responsible for making all those incorrect "Violators Will Be Towed" signs? Has anyone ever seen a towed violator? Isn't it the cars that get towed not the violators, the people who parked illegally or without the store owner's permission?

Maybe my background as a news editor makes me too picky when it comes to words, but who had the bright idea of putting big electronic signs with confusing messages over major highways? Driving into the New York City area, Irene and I looked up and saw "SIGN UNDER TEST." We debated whether that meant we should stop, look for something marked "Test" and then sign it. Were they trying to say "SIGN BEING TESTED"?

Some signs are so scary you have to take immediate action even when you're not sure exactly what they mean. In my town on Long Island, I saw a sign, "Japanese Straightening. From $199." I raced home and fired off an email to a Japanese-American I used to work with, warning him to stand tall and not slouch until this threat passed.

Is there something in the U.S. Banking Code that makes it illegal for banks to use English when dealing with customers? A statement from my bank had an entry labeled "Unrealized Market Appreciation" followed by a minus. They mean we lost money, right?

Is someone working on a class action suit to block stores from insisting we try to write our names in that tiny window in those silly boxes where you swipe your credit cards? In some of the boxes, the line where you are supposed to scribble your name is about an inch long. Who outside of Cher can do that?

How long have U.S. Air Marshals been assigned to private cars? On a summer trip with Daniella and the aforementioned chicken-fibbers who are her parents, every time I got behind the wheel there was a loud discussion (okay, disagreement) about (1) was the "air" on, (2) if so, could it be turned up higher, (3) were the vents closed, (4) if not, could they be tilted more toward the back seat and, (5) why was it always so hot when the person in charge of air, the Air Marshal, rode in front?

Do you understand the commercials you see on television? About half the time I can't understand what the people in the commercial are saying or what they are doing or what product they're trying to sell. I can't be the only one who doesn't "get" it, can I?

And does anyone know where I can get those long, black socks lots of other retired guys wear with shorts in the summer? Does Medicare send them out? I sure didn't get mine. Could they be mad at me because I didn't sign up for their drug plan?

The Good News: *I am still able to read the signs on the road and can still tell the difference between white and black socks.*

Get Ready For Some Pleasant Surprises

Look up. Over there. That woman sitting across from you doing the crossword puzzle, the one you've been living with for more than 50 years. Yes, that one. You know her—if you don't mind me getting personal—forwards and backwards, right? Know all her strengths, her every annoying habit, her every like and dislike, her every talent and skill. Don't bet on it.

Since Irene stopped working, I have learned that she plays the harmonica. Her skills on the viola, mandolin and piano I knew about. I bought, or helped buy, the latter two. The harmonica discovery came a year or so after we retired. Trying to keep our then three-year-old granddaughter, Daniella, busy and entertained, Irene opened a cabinet drawer, whipped out a harmonica and began playing *"Camp Town Races"* or some such. "Doo dah, doo dah." My eyes got wide. I used to go to business meetings where they gave away harmonicas, so there are two or three scattered around the house. But who knew Irene could play one? I didn't, her kids didn't. In the half a century I've been around her never once did she play the harmonica, talk about playing one or express a wish that she had more time to toot one.

Another discovery, again made while observing her with Daniella, is she can draw very well. Faces that look like faces, houses that look like houses. I never knew that. After realizing this, I bought her a water color painting set. As far as I know she has yet to use it. Still it wouldn't shock me if I came home one day, and her paintings were all over the wall—lighthouses in Maine, quarries in Vermont and pears, apples and grapes hanging out of fancy bowls.

The more the grandkids come over the more we will learn about her talents. Basket weaving might be one. Every couple of months I spot a new basket stuck in a corner of a room. Does she buy them or make them?

This discovery process involving your long-time mate can be a two-way street. When I mentioned once that I didn't wash my hair every day, Irene seemed amazed that it was possible to take a shower and not get your hair wet. "How do you do that?" she asked. "What are you talking about?" was my usual surly response. "Just stand so the water doesn't hit your hair. It's easy." She must think I have a really big head, in or out of the shower. I can't imagine where she got that idea.

Enjoy the discoveries. It's fun learning new things about an old buddy. I wish I hadn't told Irene years ago about playing (very badly) the sousaphone in the high school band and riding home on my bike with this silver boa constrictor wrapped around me. If I had saved that tale until now, maybe I could have persuaded her I was a real sexy dude. By 1955 standards. Nah, probably not.

The Good News: *It's great to know someone besides a politician who surprises and amazes you.*

"You've Got Some Old School Moves, Baby."

When you turn 70 you might find yourself a little more sensitive, perhaps even a little touchy, about what younger people—and there certainly are lots of 'em—say to you. One evening at a restaurant in Skaneateles, New York, a waitress asked two white-haired people—me and Irene—"Have you had enough time?"

What a nasty thing to say to two retirees who worked hard for many, many years and are out trying to have a decent meal and hoping they won't sit so long that when they get up to leave they'll have one of those not very nice farting attacks. I put the waitress in her place right fast, saying something like, "not nearly as long as we hope to have."

A similar question has been asked of me on basketball courts where I play with much younger guys, many of them teenagers. Sometimes after a game, when everyone is taking a break, one of the kids will ask, "Are you going to play another game?" My response is usually, "Do you mean today or ever?" Then I quickly add, "Yes. Give me two minutes."

Another court comment, on those rare occasions when I have played well, is that I have "old school moves." Just what the hell kind of moves am I supposed to have? When I start hearing guys tell me I have "pre-school moves," I will know it is time to throw away the sneakers.

One of the things that always sets Irene off is almost any so-called term of endearment. Waitresses are fond of calling older women "sweetheart" or "honey." Whenever that happens Irene can't talk about anything else for hours. Please stop.

"Ma'am" might make it under her radar but just barely. "Dear" and "darling" are definitely no-nos. "Hey, Lady" might even be better than any of the above. The worst word of all is "baby." At a breakfast one morning in St. Augustine, Florida, a waitress called Irene that, and I heard about it and heard about it for the next four hours as we made our way to South Carolina on what I had imagined as a relaxing, scenic ride. When we got out of the car, I wanted to call Avis and put in for Frequent Crier Miles.

The Good News: *There's nothing to stop you from turning the tables and calling the wait staff the same thing they call you and see how they like it.*

As The Doctor Says, "Now For The Fun Part."

Joke all you want about it, Guys, but I know for a fact that going to the doctor every year and letting him shove his finger up your ass pays off. That said, I do recommend you take a quick look back before he does it to make sure he's not using something else, perhaps a copy of *Sports Illustrated*.

Shortly after I turned 50 I had a TURP, an acronym for a procedure where they cram something up your kazoo and scrape away. The purpose of this amusing activity is three fold: to decrease the size of your prostate, to increase your pee stream (remember that old song "Down By The Old Pee Stream?") and to decrease the frequency of your visits to the bathroom. Having to take a leak every 30 minutes ain't normal, Chester.

My TURP accomplished all three, and after that there were yearly checkups, including the much loved FUTA (Finger Up The Ass), PSA blood tests and urine samples. All was fine until one December when I was told I had prostate cancer. The doctor outlined my options and gave me some material to read. I quickly contacted other guys who had had prostate cancer, one of them my older brother Jim, a retired Southern Baptist minister. Jim and I were good buddies growing up and did everything together; paper routes, playing all kinds of ball, swimming, hanging out, and even going on a few dates together—(with girls, not each other).

In talking to Jim about what had been done about his prostate cancer and how happy he was with the results, he casually uttered a word I had never heard from his lips before. "Erections." Holy shit!

When you get to be our age you realize, finally, that talking out loud about a good old "hard-on" isn't going to kill you. When the subject is your health problems or someone else's, you drop all that bashful, squeamish business and just say whatever it is. Another prostate cancer survivor, someone I have never met, sent me an email in which he talked about orgasms, past and present.

Loosen up, Guys. Bend over and let the doctor do his work, and, if the news turns out bad, ask around for suggestions and advice.

With that in mind, I've put together a little Q & A about things I learned before, during and after 45 radiation sessions.

Q: Why does most medical literature describe the prostate as a gland "about the size of a walnut?"

A: Because the Red Plum Growers' Cooperative spent big bucks on a first-rate P.R. agency to keep plums from being linked with prostates, leaving the Walnut Farmers of America more or less holding their own you know whats.

Q: The PSA is a test frequently used to detect the possibility of prostate cancer. What does PSA stand for?

A: Please Say Ah.

Q: What is a PSA rating?

A: In laymen's terms, it simply means how good your "ah" is during and after urination.

Q: How are PSA ratings taken?

A: Mini-cameras hidden in the bathrooms where you are told to go to go.

Q: What is a good PSA rating?

A: This is one of those cases where PG 13 is bad, real bad. In this numbers game, the lower the PSA rating, the better. This isn't the NBA where you're hoping for a three-pointer. A PSA rating of one or less is excellent. Three is not so hot.

Q: Why don't women have prostates?

A: Because they're smarter than men.

Q: Let's say I have a PSA rating of four or higher and the doctor tells me he wants to do a biopsy of the prostate. How does he do that?

A: Brace yourself. He shoots staples into the prostate. YOUR prostate.

Q: Why?

A: Partly because it's fun and also because the staples remove small pieces of the prostate for further tests.

Q: Does it hurt?

A: Next question.

Q: How do you feel after a prostate biopsy?

A: Like hurrying home, grabbing your staple gun and running your car over it and then going next door and asking your neighbor to start up his Hummer and do it again, just to make sure.

Q: What should I do if I live in a big city and don't have a staple gun or a car?

A: Buy a staple gun anyway, check on what time the garbage truck comes by and then throw it in the street right on schedule.

Q: What happens if the biopsy shows traces of cancer?

A: The doctor will call you in for consultation, and, if you've been having regular checkups, he likely will tell you right off that you probably aren't going to die from this.

Q: Should I believe him?

A: Of course. You still have money in the bank, right? He will suggest ways he can get some of it.

Q: What sort of ways?

A: Well, he'll outline several options. Doing nothing but carefully monitoring the situation. Or various radiation treatments, including seeds which they implant in the prostate. Some patients aren't all that thrilled with seeds because of the frequent watering involved to help them grow. There's chemotherapy. Removing your prostate.

Q: Removing the prostate? They take it out? Do they put something in its place?

A: Normally they don't, but I suppose there's no harm in asking if they could slip a walnut back up there.

To repeat: Go to your doctor and let him do his thing and your thing at the same time.

It's worth the little bit of discomfort. And talking about erections isn't all that boring. It sure beats listening to some blowhard on TV spouting off about exit polls.

The Good News: *Never once when you were growing up did you say to yourself, "You know what— I'd like to stick my finger up other guys' asses for a living."*

Go Ahead. Help In The Kitchen But Don't Expect Any Medals.

You may want to start helping out more around mealtime—something beyond taking a seat or putting the pepper mill on the table—and maybe even cook dinner occasionally, but be aware there are dangers involved. They include verbal artillery and hovercraft.

I fixed lamb burgers one night, along with onions, zucchini and carrots in a second skillet, while Irene was in charge of making the couscous. It was a real team effort and tasty, I thought. When we were almost finished, I made a silly joke about how nicely I sliced the carrots and socko—she let me have it. Anytime a woman begins a sentence with the word "only" you know there is about to be incoming verbal artillery.

"Only next time," Irene chided, "put the carrots in before the onions and zucchini. It takes carrots longer to cook." As much as it hurt, she did have a point. The zucchini was a little mushy.

Before retirement I did some simple, non-adventurous cooking. Basically meat balls, meat loaf, fried chicken, *coq au vin* (easy to make despite the fancy name), pork chops and apple pie. Within days after I stopped working, my daughter Julie, a wonderful cook, gave me a large bottle of bourbon, the best-seller, *Why Do Men Have Nipples?* and two cookbooks. The cookbooks I suspect were really for the benefit of her mother who was still working and counting on me to have supper going when she got home.

My first effort from the cookbooks was a dried fruit bread with olive oil and pine nuts. It looked pretty, but Irene wasn't impressed. "It didn't rise. It's awfully flat. Did you put baking powder in it?" No, I said, because the recipe didn't call for baking powder. Trusting nothing I say, she walked over to the cookbook to check for herself. We were both right. It didn't call for baking powder, and it didn't rise.

Vegetarian lasagna, prepared from one of the books, also wasn't a smash hit. Irene remained silent about what she was eating until her plate was nearly empty. "Well, I guess we stick with meat." That recipe has never been tried again by either of us.

Other times, in making something more familiar to us both, I was told I was using the "wrong pan." My dream is to win Power Ball and take part of the money to start my own business, The Right Pan Company, unless someone has beaten me to the punch. To all assertions that I had used the wrong pan, I nodded or grunted and sometimes even chuckled. Past experience had shown that when this allegation was made the food did, somehow, cook in the wrong damn pan, and we then ate it and lived to talk about it. So what's the big deal?

Don't get discouraged. Should there be incoming verbal artillery along the lines of "when I make chicken cutlets, I always . . . ," smile and say "really." Do not, under any circumstances, say "no shit." Do try to distract her. "You know, my little radish," you might begin, "I wouldn't stand too close to the stove. It made a very funny noise a couple of minutes ago. The tappets may be loose. I thought you were watching a movie in the front room?" Resist the temptation to throw a pan at her. It would be the wrong pan anyway. She does appreciate, or says she does, your efforts, clumsy as they may be, so be patient with her. She is adjusting too. You have invaded her space.

Also once you volunteer to cook and the offer is accepted, be prepared for hovercraft visits. The lady in your life will say she just came into the kitchen to get a drink of water or more ice for her drink. Bullshit! She's dying to see how bad the pot roast looks, how big of a mess you are making (on the floor, the counters, the ceiling) and how many wrong pans and utensils you have dirtied.

Even if you get pretty good at one thing—I lucked into a terrific, never-fail pie crust recipe—your old pal will feel it's her duty to make sure you don't drop the ball. One Thanksgiving I offered to make two pies, a mincemeat and a pumpkin. When the mincemeat crust was ready, the HMS Irene Hovercraft sailed into the kitchen and started fussing with the pie. When asked what the hell she thought she was doing, she said she was there to "repair" the crust. After the pumpkin filling was made and poured into the crust, more hovering. This time she was "rescuing" the crust. She does have a better eye for what makes a pie crust more attractive and inviting, so I should be thankful that the captain of the hovercraft doubles as Saint Irene, Rescuer of Wayward Crusts.

Slick magazines portray cooking as a sensual experience with luscious food and fine wine in thin glasses leading to tempting silk sheets and great pleasures. You're too old to fall for that baloney. One night I fixed a whole chicken, rubbed lovingly and tenderly with olive oil. Alongside the chicken were potatoes, whole garlic, eggplant and red bell peppers. As we took the chicken out of the oven, I, in my wisdom, said, "Look how the legs are spread, inviting entry." Not a word in reply. Just one of those looks, the kind you get in real life, not the kind you see in expensive magazines. Women, who always claim they like guys with a sense of humor, take the kitchen pretty seriously, but it would do them good to see the fun we're having making them feel oh so nervous.

The Good News: *Even when you fix something that turns out truly awful, she won't say, "You don't expect me to eat this crap, do you?"*

The Locker Room

The gym is now one of your best friends. You'll spend as much time there as you can. It gets you out of the house, keeps you from getting under foot or into trouble. And it's good for you. Should you use the locker room to shower after your workout, you will realize, once again, that your mother was right: naked men do the strangest things. I suppose one or two guys on my high school football team might have looked good in the buff, but the truth is most males don't—certainly not after age 25, regardless of how much we exercise. Without benefit of clothing, 95.99% of us look like either a huge wad of bubble gum or a giant Milk Dud.

That's why it's so astonishing—to me, anyway—that so many men do such private things in public without a stitch on. Shaving, for instance. A close shave with a hand razor is about as personal as it gets—invigorating but impossible to do with any elegance. It's a real rigmarole involving: **face**—covered with foam—pushed to within two inches of the mirror; **neck** tilted up exposing an autobahn of throat; **mouth** ajar with the size and shape of the opening constantly changing; **nose** bent (left, right and up, although never simultaneously) and **head** swiveled in every direction, hoping, vainly, for better light.

At my gym you can't miss these *au naturel* shaving performances. They are staged in front of a very large mirror in a very small locker room.

Après shave can be another major production. One gent puts on five or six lotions and then wanders around talking to the attendant or anyone who will pretend to listen, stopping occasionally to look up at a business show on television—still wearing nothing. (I've never looked down there, but I wonder if things rise and fall in sync with the Dow Jones Industrial Averages.)

After using a hair dryer, he eventually gets dressed. Next comes the real "interesting part." He strolls back to the mirror where he combs and combs and combs—the skin on his head. Except for a laughable horseshoe around his ears, he has no hair. Does he not know this? What does he think he is combing?

On odd occasions the hair dryers are employed for odd chores. I have seen a naked man stand in front of the shaving mirror with a dryer trained on his cheeks—the ones attached to his ass.

Some guys are sitters who lounge around in the nude for long periods, reading the paper or staring at the television. I don't believe they're gay, hoping to attract anyone interested. I think they're merely flat-out strange.

Then there are the grunters who grunt and sigh nonstop while undressing after exercising; the sprayers who hit you and anything within 50 feet when putting on hairspray or deodorant; and the Guardians of the Arch who get out of the shower clothes-less and clueless and dry themselves with a towel while standing under the arch dividing the locker and the shower areas. They make it impossible for anyone to get around them in either direction.

You may decide after seeing all this weird behavior that you will skip the locker room and rush home to shower. After years of membership at the same gym, the biggest surprise to me is that some marketing guru hasn't brought out a version of Burma Shave just for locker rooms.

He always shaved
Without his britches.

And after the tornado
He needed many stitches.
Naked Shave.

The Good News: *If you remember to keep your glasses off until you're ready to leave the locker room, you won't have to witness most of this.*

"Would You Like To See The Dessert Menu?"

Columbus may have discovered America, but, by golly, I've discovered something nearly as important. Lunch! For more than 40 years I ate lunch at my desk at work. It was almost always simple and quick and eaten hurriedly. In a newsroom there was usually a story or a tip that needed chasing, so I kept working while devouring a yogurt with a bag of peanuts swished around in it, followed by an orange or apple. In later years my menu switched to an unbuttered hard roll and an apple or orange. On days when there was a major story before lunchtime, I didn't eat. There wasn't time. Coffee was the fuel that kept me going.

Now, more than five years after my last deadline, I'm convinced nothing beats eating lunch out. It's the pace that makes it special. The restaurants don't have the music blaring. There aren't people at the bar who have been there since last Thursday, getting tanked up and cruder every sipping second. You don't have to worry about how you're dressed as long as you have on a clean shirt and pants. You aren't told it will be a 45 minute wait and handed a beeper too big to stick into your pants (or underwear), which, when it finally goes off, will make you nearly wet yourself.

Going to lunch is one wonderful relaxing hour and a half. You can have a glass of wine, take your time, talk to your lunch companion, look at the dessert menu for ten minutes or more and decide to split something or skip it altogether.

The proportions are smaller so you eat less. Much of the day is still ahead so you drink less. You don't leave feeling stuffed and bloated, afraid to look in a shop window because you know damn well you will see a reflection of Orson Welles.

Lunch with Irene is special, even at a very casual place. That's probably because I did shift work for years, and that meant the only time we ate together was on my days off. Now we frequently head out the door on the spur of the moment, arranged by an exchange of emails from downstairs where she works to my work room upstairs. I got this message recently in my inbox:

> "How about a quick lunch at Panera? Thought about fixing myself an egg sandwich . . . but the idea didn't especially appeal to me . . . and it's too cold for yogurt."

And off we went. We had a nice relaxing meal—soups and salads—got out of the house, saw different faces, heard different voices. All positive things.

Our favorite place for lunch is JoJo Apples, a 15 to 20 minute drive, about four blocks from the Atlantic Ocean. It has very good food, lots to choose from, reasonable prices, and a friendly small town atmosphere. They also serve breakfast all day, and for grandparents with two pancake-loving granddaughters that's hard to beat. We can take Daniella and Cristiana to lunch, and they can have their pancakes while Irene has salmon on greens and I have a veggie wrap or the walnut and apple salad. Plus, when we're done, we all know that a mile down the road is the best ice cream place around.

Lunch is the ideal venue for getting together with a former co-worker. You trade war stories, catch up on what each of you has been doing (translation: what kind of doctors the two of you have seen lately) and play "whatever happened to" Bob What's his name and Jill What's her face. Be forewarned though that "whatever happened to" can be a little upsetting when you don't remember half the people the other person is talking about. Worse yet is when you don't have the dimmest recollection of some ridiculous thing the person sitting across from you laughing his or her ass off alleges you did or said. In such circumstances, it's permissible to rise from your seat and lean over to get a real close look at your old work buddy to make sure you didn't confuse your dates. It could be that you are lunching with a former copy editor at ABC News in New York, when for an hour now you had thought this was an ex-boss from Radio Free Europe in Munich. That could explain why you were having such a hell of a time getting a fix on most of the names being thrown out at you.

Like anything else there are times when lunch can be a bummer. That's usually when you get stuck agreeing to meet a former co-worker you were never all that thrilled about. When this person said "let's have lunch next Tuesday," you, for some inexplicable reason, jumped at the offer and said "yes."

What makes this outing so painful is that the other person never shuts up. He or she does all the talking. All of it. After the meaningless, "Hi, how are you?" and the handshake or hug, he or she is off and running. These jabber mouths are impervious. I swear if you said to them, "The doctor told me last week I have only one ball. It has now worked its way up into my left bicep. Want me to show you?" their response would be, "Oh, really. No kidding. As I was saying . . . ."

You're never too old to learn. This is one of those times. When next this creature phones or emails about lunch, you are suddenly one very, very busy son of a bitch and totally unavailable.

The Good News: *In six months you're allowed to change your mind about never having lunch again with the annoying former co-worker, if they make it clear they will pick up the check this time.*

For Men Only

In a perfect world this chapter would be printed in a special ink visible only to male eyes. I can only get in trouble for writing it. The same goes for any man caught reading it, and that's why I'll keep it as short as possible. Since this has really happened to me, I feel an obligation to pass on this information in case you are faced with a similar situation where you can't stop laughing but refuse to give the Mrs. any hint what set you off.

Be prepared, as the Boy Scouts say, to be driving on a fine, sunny day and look over at your companion and realize she is someone else, someone you have never met. I'm not talking about a knockout from either yesterday or today—a Sophia Loren or an Angelina Jolie. I mean someone you would never think of.

My wife (I don't dare use her name here) has kinky hair, which gets kinkier as the temperature rises. On the day in question—a hot summer day—she had on a new pair of sunglasses, big ones, aviator style.

We are talking about nothing in particular when I look over to the passenger seat, and I'll be damned if Carl Perkins isn't sitting there. Curly hair, sunglasses and all. I'm married to Carl Perkins! The guy who wrote "Blue Suede Shoes." Me and Carl Perkins are an item! I start laughing but refuse to tell my no-name wife what's so funny. How could I? What would I say? "You know, whatever your name is, with your kinky hair and those big sunglasses you look exactly like Carl Perkins!" And then maybe hum a few bars of, "uh-uh, Honey, lay off of my shoes." I don't think so. I do not have a death wish.

It was my one and only sighting of Carl, but I'll never forget it. Thank you. Mr. Perkins. My wife, who will again be identified in subsequent chapters, obviously didn't see Carl nor did I give her a chance to see this chapter before I sent it to the publisher. Otherwise we might have separate Zip Codes now.

The Good News: *Thank God, I didn't look over and see Lawrence Welk.*

"No Messages"

When America was strong and generally well-liked around the world, we had TV sets that you walked up to and turned on. It was a simple, efficient one knob process. Now we sit on our asses with remotes in our hands and press a bunch of buttons before anything happens. At my house we have satellite television, which means you need to push buttons five times to get a picture. That ain't progress, Cecil.

"It's too damn complicated," I angrily say to Irene every time I forget to push the buttons in the right sequence and end up with either a bright, blue screen or a salt and pepper one with a very loud churning sound that would scare the shit out of Helen Keller. At this point Irene usually takes over while I continue to mutter, "it's too damn complicated." (Full disclosure: My actual words are much more colorful.) Sometimes one of us manages to get things so bollixed up that we call our son, Jack, who is always very helpful and lives seven minutes away.

The biggest challenge comes every three months or so when, because of a storm on Long Island or perhaps a low water level on the Ganges, the satellite dish and our TV set get out of whack and need to be realigned. Or something. Jack has walked us through this process a hundred times. We have taken notes as he explained that there are numbers you have to enter into the remote, where you find those numbers and how to enter them. But, of course, when we need the notes, we can't find them nor the book with the numbers in it. As I understand it, once the notes and the numbers are located you place three heavy towels on the floor, stand at least ten feet away from them, then enter the first two numbers, pivot, sing the first three lines from "If I Were A Rich Man," wiggle your butt as fast as you can while facing due west (or is it east?), and enter the next two numbers while pressing the On-Off, TV and SAT buttons simultaneous with your thumbs and the middle finger of either hand. The final step is to pray to the God of your choice.

Jack has become our chief TV maintenance man because (a) he has the same service, (b) he's a good son who knows we are helpless, and (c) he doesn't charge for house calls if you exclude the occasional bourbon and Coke after he has resolved our latest conundrum.

It's embarrassing to keep calling companies with problems that you or someone you know should be able to quickly figure out. A few years back, before we began relying exclusively on Jack, a TV set in the breakfast nook had been out of commission (blue screen disease) for more than a month. After a satellite dish employee spent many minutes on the phone unsuccessfully trying to help us find a solution, it was agreed that we needed a hands-on professional. When the technician showed up, I immediately confessed, "I'm an idiot." He left, I'm confident, knowing I am a man of my word. It took him six seconds to discover that the wrong button was depressed on the top of the set. In this age of remotes who would have ever thought of looking there for the problem? When the technician and his buddies get together after work, they must have some genuinely funny stories about the likes of us. Old people do have a useful purpose: bringing humor into the lives of handymen and women across the country.

I've learned, as you have or will, not to question younger people when they talk about TV sets, cell phones or computers. I don't want to brag, but I'm surprisingly facile with a cell phone and that includes text messaging. Yes, I hit the wrong buttons sometimes, but I get the job done and don't use any abbreviations, so that slows me down some. A few times I have screwed up to the point that the keypad on the cell phone locked up on me. Not to worry. I pick up an old-fashioned telephone to track down one of the older grandkids and they always get me out of my mess.

I also rely on Nicholas or Rachel when I run into computer problems. Many times they know the answer, sometimes they don't. But if you are having trouble storing something on your computer and a ten-year-old grandchild says, "Why don't you put it on your hard drive?" don't argue. Do as you're told or smarter yet, ask the young advice-giver to do it for you. They, after all, know what they're doing. Too bad the grandkids have to go to school or aren't around when I turn on the computer in the morning and a box appears on the screen saying my version of Adolf the Acrobat—or whatever it is called—is outdated and click here for an Update. I usually click as instructed and always wonder later if I really had to.

If you're like me, sophisticated cars are another constant mystery. For more than two years, we have owned one of the cheapest Volvos they sell, and occasionally when I turn on the ignition a sign appears on the dashboard saying, "NO MESSAGES." That's good, I say to myself. I don't know what I would do if there were a message. What sort of message would it be? Am I going to get into the car someday and the sign on the dashboard will read, "EAT MORE PORK," or "AT&T SUCKS." Or "YOU DIDN'T FLOSS."

Who wants to bet some genius is trying to talk the car makers into selling that space on the dash for advertising? That would be real nice, wouldn't it? I'm so out of touch that for all I know it's already being done.

There are too many gadgets and sensors on our Volvo, too many things that can go wrong. I do give the Swedes a pat on the behind for putting heaters under the front seats. On a cool morning or after a day of skiing, a warm seat feels good on these old bones. Yo, Swedish engineers, as they say in your country, "tack så mycket." (I sure hope that means "thank you very much" and not "squeeze my herring.")

The Good News: *The message on the dashboard has yet to read "THE END IS NEAR."*

GPS = Getting Places Simply = No Adventures

The one time you want to ignore the technical advice of the kids and grandkids is when they pester you about buying a Global Positioning System receiver for your car. Don't be bullied into this. You've gotten along fine without one for years. You don't need it.

Yes, a GPS device can be set so you travel from point A, your house, to point B, your destination, quickly and without hassle. That's great if you're a delivery man or a person in a hurry. But you're neither. You don't have a job or a rigid schedule. You're old. Retired. Save your money.

GPS lovers don't understand that some of us hate going directly from point A to point B. How boring is that? Count me among those who don't mind taking the long way around. In fact, I enjoy it. There's nothing in the world wrong with not knowing exactly where you are at times. Columbus sure didn't, and he wouldn't have his own national holiday if he were regarded by historians as just another schmuck with a boat.

GPS owners are like robots. They go on programmed trips. We GPS-less Marco Polos go on adventures. We discover the most fascinating towns, streets, houses, dead ends and people, all by pure chance. We missed a turn, got on the wrong road, or decided to ignore our dog-eared map and headed down an interesting-looking street that could end up being a short cut but in all likelihood won't.

Sure you can start out from your house in Merrick, New York, and punch in your destination—Blue Hill at Stone Barns, Pocantico Hills, New York (or is it Blue Barns at Stone Hill?)—and cruise smartly into the parking lot one hour and ten minutes later after a stress-free drive. But before you get all that damn smug think of all you missed:

Did you have a chance to practice your U-turns on the drive from Merrick to Blue Barns at Hill Stone? A good trip should include at least eight U-turns, three or four made within seconds of each other.

Did you meet any strangers along the way, people who smirked when you said you were looking for Stoned Blue at Barnes & Noble, people who talk real slowly, spacing their words about a month apart, people who said, after looking at each other in a mischievous way, "Boy, are you ever lost."

Did you see on your left, at one point, a large body of water or a well-known church, and then, after driving 57 very slow miles that left you needing a bathroom break really, really bad, realize that by God that large body of water or well-known church was now suddenly on your right?

Did your navigator announce her resignation many miles and hours ago? Is she sitting beside you mute and frowning as though auditioning for a part in a silent movie? (She'll get over it. Or at least she always has before.)

Those of us who drive without the help of electronic navigational aids enjoy the trip along the way. And once we arrive, finally, we have something to remember. Arguments. Unmarked streets. Detours and other surprises. Upset stomachs. More unmarked streets. A huge north-south Interstate that appears to have been built without a single entrance for people who want to go south. The first words spoken by the navigator after, apparently, rescinding her resignation.

What do drivers armed with GPS take away from an uncomplicated, problem-free trip to point B? Not much. Certainly no ammunition for stories that are funny a few weeks—make that months—later.

Early one fall morning Irene and I headed east on Long Island to pick up the daughter of a friend, a high school senior who had an interview scheduled at Sarah Lawrence College in Bronxville, New York. Jack, a freelance photographer who genuinely needs GPS to make sure he arrives on time at unfamiliar locations, insisted on loaning us his system. He stuck it on our windshield the night before and gave Irene a five-minute course on how to operate it along with a set of written instructions.

As we drove east to Bay Shore, Long Island, both Irene and I looked occasionally at the map on the GPS screen, which kept changing. After our young lady passenger got into the car, I pushed a button on the side of the GPS and the map disappeared, never to be seen again. This to me was an obvious signal that we were off to a good start.

Irene fooled around with the GPS a while, pushing this or that icon on the screen. It refused to cooperate, but we didn't need its help. A MapQuest print out we brought with us showed that Sarah Lawrence was near the road I take when going to the Catskills to ski. We pulled into a parking lot at Sarah Lawrence at 8:15, one hour and 15 minutes before the young lady's interview.

Irene and I laughed. We had somehow screwed up the GPS but still arrived way ahead of time. We knew that Jack would be amazed, yet again, and very annoyed, yet again, with our incompetence and our lackadaisical view of the value of electronic gadgets. "He's going to kill us," we kept saying and then giggling.

On the drive back to Long Island, the high school senior thought she might know how to get the GPS out of its non-functioning, uncooperative mode. She suggested that Irene type the words "Bay Shore" on the key pad and tried it herself a time or two from the back seat. These combined efforts produced a listing of various towns named "Bay Side." Irene and I joked about calling Jack to tell him we love the GPS, love it so much we have decided to drive with it to Bay Side, California. As predicted, he was not amused when we relayed details of our latest "adventure."

He feels we needlessly take the longest route possible and are always getting, as he so crudely puts it, "lost." So? Because we aren't constantly worried about where we are or exactly where we are going, we have stumbled upon sections of the Erie Canal, terrific little restaurants, museums, stunning homes, galleries, lovely little towns, very old cemeteries, parks, lakes, rivers and on and on.

Jack has benefited from these meanderings. Years ago while driving around, in circles probably, in southern Vermont we came upon a farm with cans of maple syrup for sale. About twice a year since then, we have sent a blank check to Mr. Truman Young for more of his wonderful syrup. Not only do Jack and his family love it, his in-laws do too. Keeping the in-laws happy is important.

Irene and I looked for the farm on subsequent trips but lucked into finding it only one other time. We know it's out there somewhere. The important thing is that the mailman knows where it is, takes our checks there and Mr. Young's syrup ends up on our table. As far as I'm concerned, that's mission accomplished.

The Good News: *The old, non-electronic way of doing things is sometimes better and almost always "funner."*

Sex
(Or A Reasonable Facsimile Thereof)

Here's a news flash. It takes longer to do things these days, including you know what. Ah, life is so unfair. Imagine the thrills you would have had at 23 if it took you as long then to have an orgasm as it does at 70. It's a shame, as George Bernard Shaw said, that "youth is wasted on the young."

But sex can be mighty fine in your 70s, and one reason is there are a hell of a lot fewer distractions. The office isn't going to call you about a problem anyone with a smidgen of common sense could handle on his own. You don't face the choice between having an orgasm and missing the train. The kids aren't going to barge in, and even if they did they might applaud instead of screaming and running away like the last time 35 years ago. In short, you can take your sweet time enjoying things.

Theoretically, you have all day to finish the task at hand, although let's hope it doesn't come to that. I suspect many of us old guys, with or without chemical supplements, have devised our own methods of achieving satisfaction. If it works for you, who's to criticize it?

It's best not to let your mind wander though. In my own case, orgasm has been difficult, if not impossible to achieve, if I got sidetracked into thinking about:

- Office supplies. Staplers, chairs, computer cartridges and the like.
- Whether to order the harvest salad or the Portobello tower the next time we go out to lunch.

- The first three digits of the phone number at our first apartment in Chicago.
- Whether pickles and olives are in aisle 3 or aisle 7 at the supermarket.
- The name of that terrific bridge leading to downtown Savannah.

We are old enough to know that if we keep our thoughts focused on what we are doing and yet nothing happens, it's not the end of the world. It just seems like it for an hour or so.

Should your partner be unreceptive after many years of good sex, here are some things you could try.

- Begging.
- Buy sex tapes. Not many people know it, but Abbott and Costello made a sex instruction film, "Who Goes First?" that takes you from step a to step b. There are only two steps, aren't there? It's not as funny as "Who's On First?" but much more useful.
- Buy a parakeet and train it to talk dirty.
- Begging.
- Promise to do something she has been nagging you about for months. A closet that needs cleaning out, according to her, or a home repair that, unskilled as you are, you still might be able to do. If worst comes to worst, agree to watch with her one of those stupid reality TV programs she likes and can't stop talking about.
- When you're "in the mood," drop a few hints about how good the ugliest woman neighbor, friend or acquaintance you can think of looked the other day at the mall.
- Begging.

None of this may work and then you're truly screwed.

The Good News: *Although its frequency has diminished (you do remember the last time, I trust), sex at 70 remains as enjoyable and as mysterious as ever.*

What Rhymes With Wars and Whores?

"Chores" is an awful word with a terrible sound to it. Listen to what it rhymes with:

Wars
Whores
Sores
Bores
Snores
Gores

There's nothing good to be said about chores, yet as a retiree you've lost most legitimate reasons for avoiding the blasted things. On a gorgeous day when you've had lunch and a nap and spent the last two hours unsuccessfully trying to rewrite one short paragraph, there are no persuasive alibis for why you are totally unavailable to, say, fill the planter boxes with dirt, lug them up to the deck and position them on the railings.

For nearly 30 years I got out of being asked to help around the house because of one brilliant display of maturity, aptitude and temper. I was asked to "take a look at"—I presume that meant to "fix"—a bookcase in Jack's room, which had been assembled, disassembled and reassembled several times in our various moves. I trudged up to the attic, Jack's room at the time, in no mood to waste time on something as menial as repairing a bookcase, especially one that wouldn't stand up straight. It leaned badly to the right and the shelves sagged. I tried for maybe three or four minutes to get the shelves and various pieces to—in the words of our Founding Fathers—"form a more perfect union."

It was soon clear that this was beyond my capabilities in carpentry, not to mention patience. I got frustrated, lost it and kicked and pounded the bookcase apart. The disparate elements were soon transported to the basement. All these years later I still firmly believe the trip to the attic was a huge success. I did the job assigned me. I fixed it. We never had a problem with that bookcase again.

After this when Irene mentioned, "I wish we could do something about" X, I would volunteer to repair it but was quickly told, "That's okay, that's okay." Now, with no train to catch, no phone calls from work, no compelling reason why I must read closely every national and international story in the newspapers, I am called upon occasionally to help with % ^ &*(&*(O)P! chores, particularly in the garden.

I shouldn't really mind. I like our house and garden so I ought to take some pride in ownership and the obligations that come with it. But I frequently get annoyed mid-chore when I realize once again that, for all her talents, Irene can't count. At breakfast she will say, "Sometime today I'd like you to help me move a couple of plants. I need you to dig some holes." A time for this endeavor is agreed upon, I appear on the deck, work gloves are offered and away we go. Dig, dig, dig.

Once I have dug enough holes for two plants, a "couple," Irene informs me, "There are a couple of others I could use some help with." This second, surprise "couple," is in fact, at a minimum, another four but normally at least six or eight. It's good we don't have a busy social life, or we would never have enough bourbon or Stoli to go around when Irene invites a "couple" of people over for drinks.

I'm frequently guilty of a similar misinterpretation

when Irene says, "I'd like to stop at Home Depot. I need top soil." In parsing that first sentence, "stop" to me means a brief cessation of motion, a quick in and out at a store. No loitering, no meandering from aisle to aisle gawking at door handles, barbecue sets, garden gadgets, doohickeys, tape measures and hickeydoos. It seems to me that a reasonable understanding of the second sentence— "I need top soil"—is that we will run in, head straight to the top soil zone, grab a few bags, put them in a cart, race to the checkout line and we are out of there. Why am I always so wrong about this?

Either on the way to or from the top soil section, Irene discloses she also needs some cell packs, those little plastic boxes with sprouts in them. Shopping for these tiny devils is complicated and oh so time consuming. Each cell pack must be lifted up, looked at, turned 360 degrees, put back down, before there's a loud sigh and the process repeats itself. (No, I don't know what the sigh is about.) There are all kinds of would-be flowers in cell packs. Some don't look right, some are too expensive ("I'm not paying $3.99 for that!"), and the store has always sold out of one kind that she wanted, which means cell packs previously lifted, looked at, turned 360 degrees and rejected for whatever reason undergo close scrutiny again, and may, if they behave themselves, make it into the shopping cart. In short, this stop at Home Depot eats up a good hour of mine and the Lord's time.

One chore I don't complain much about involves piles. No, not that kind—rather the clumps of grass, weeds, twigs and rocks Irene has left in the yard after raking. Without any previous warning, I will see the piles when I come home from wherever and spend the next few minutes putting them in plastic bags or a garbage can. No problem. It's mindless and that's why Irene considers me qualified to handle it. That's not her attitude about my skill level when it comes to one of the biggest chores of the week—grocery shopping. But as you will soon see, she's the one who doesn't know beans about that.

The Good News: *Raking leaves can be a sign that winter isn't far off and that means no more yard work for you until spring.*

Voiding The Void

Having made very good money as a stock boy for a large grocery store chain during my first two years of college, I retain a fondness for supermarkets. With more free time than ever before, I like to go in and grade them. Are the canned goods neatly arranged at the front of the shelves, are the aisles clear of boxes or other obstacles that make it hard for customers to get around, is the produce section neat and appealing, are the male employees wearing ties and are the knots properly tied? Irene also worked in a grocery store, during high school, but never for a real national biggie. Maybe that's why she seems lost in a large supermarket.

She usually has a list of what we need and looks at it when we enter the door of our local store where the produce section is the first thing you see. She will pick out some fruit or greens and notice that aluminum foil is next on her list and walk three aisles over to get it and then return to the produce area for onions and potatoes. She will tell me to, "Get whatever juice you want" and off I go to the juice aisle while she heads for the meat counter. After deciding on a package of ground beef and a pork roast, she will spot paper towels on the list and go back two aisles to get them. She backtracks to the meat counter for chicken cutlets and maybe then heads all the way over to the juice aisle to get her own juice before retracing her steps for a package of bacon. This back and forth goes on so often I sometimes feel Irene thinks these stores are called circle markets.

Those times when I am authorized to go to the circle market on my own the comments on my return are as predictable as the tides. I always, according to Irene, buy the most expensive brands and, the sin of sins, never notice what's on sale. As a devoted reader of grocery store fliers in the newspapers, she may know that Ronzoni linguini is on sale for TWO boxes for $1.99, while I paid almost that much for one box of brand Z. Fair enough. But indulge me as I relay a story of her idea of a bargain, recounted in a letter to a niece a few years back while I was still employed.

> I got home today around 3 p.m., washed my face, brushed my teeth and off we went to the supermarket. As we wander through the aisles, Irene, the Hungarian-Protestant, tells me, the Scots-Irish, that if we spend over $50 we get a free box of Passover matzos. We McCoys, of course, celebrate Passover endlessly and obviously go through a lot of matzos. We simply can't get enough of them.
>
> When we get to the dairy-bread aisle, Irene picks up this small box of matzos and asks me to read the fine print on the coupon she has for the free matzos. The coupon says the free matzos come in a five-pound box. The matzo box I'm holding in my hand probably weighs six ounces, tops. So she, the big matzo eater, goes looking for a manager. The next time I see her she is at the other end of the aisle with this enormous box of Passover matzos. The package says there are five (5) one pound (1 lb.) boxes of matzos in this thing, enough matzos to last the matzo-loving McCoys until roughly 2077.
>
> This is nuts. There are two (2) of us. We will never eat all this. But do I say anything? Of course not. We've been married for 45 years, and I know not to say a word. We go to the checkout counter, and I start bagging as I always do. It's fun. Reminds me of my college A&P days. The kid checking us

out—Brian it says on his name tag—seems to be new, which is excellent because the Hungarian-Protestant is about to give him a real work out. I have everything bagged except the Passover matzos when Irene, an avid register watcher, says, 'Oh, you mean that's $4.99? I thought the coupon said it was free.' Ah, the magic word, 'free.'

Brian handles it well. Very cool. He is instructed to take the matzos off our bill and asks the young lady running the adjacent checkout counter to help him void the purchase. She does, but she tells him the matzos are, in fact, free. Hearing this, Irene says she wants them, which for Brian means he has to void the void. Like I say, he's cool. He's not flustered, doesn't appear to be aggravated, but, being new, he doesn't know how to void a void. After conferring again with the checker next to him, it's decided he needs to summon a supervisor. One eventually appears, and there is conversation about all of the above among the participants, focusing on whether 'free' really means free. Once that is out of the way, the void is voided. Yes! Amen! We'll soon be on our way home.

But wait. Although we haven't paid yet, I excuse myself and push the cart out to the parking lot, unload four full grocery bags into the trunk of the Cabrio and get behind the wheel. No Irene. I see her standing in the checkout line, talking. She is not normally a talker. When she finally emerges from the store, she is smiling. SHE GOT A FIVE-POUND BOX OF PASSOVER MATZOS FOR FREE!

She explains, as I stare into the distance, that the final delay in this marvelous transaction was caused by her decision to pay in cash, something *we rarely do, and Brian—he should have won the Employee of the Month Award right on the spot for his patience—didn't have any change. If I were a brave man, I would try to imagine what he told his folks about all this when he went home.*

My recollection is that we two matzo gluttons may have eaten, in a span of six months or more, one of the five boxes of matzos. The other four I'm certain ended up you know where. Yes, the matzos were free, but if Irene were really a hotshot supermarket shopper wouldn't she have been on Martha Stewart's show by now?

The Good News: *I can't remember us ever bringing home another box of matzos, free or otherwise.*

Fadeaway Jump Shots And Fading Memories

I'm very fortunate. Although I'm over 70, I'm still able to play basketball and frequently get invited by much younger guys to join them in pickup games. As a senior citizen, I know my place in life and on the court. I don't drive to the basket like the youngsters who enjoy crashing into each other. I stay 15 to 17 feet away and take jump shots. Some days I do okay, other days I really stink. But hey, that's exactly how things were when I was working.

I can't play as long as I used to and always say "no" these days to full-court games. That doesn't bother me. I still love the action. What is troubling though is an inability to recognize people I once knew so well. One recent summer afternoon a young man greeted me with a "hello" when I arrived at the court, walked over to shake my hand and said, "Hi, Larry. How you doing? How's your son?" A week or so later another young man did the same thing. Both times I didn't have a clue who these guys were.

One of them remembered that I grew up in Indiana and went to Indiana University. He kept talking and I kept drawing blanks. Finally, I said, "Help me. What's your name?" He told me and still no bells went off. Perhaps if Jack had been there he could have provided some hints, something about the guy or his game that would have triggered my memory cells.

When Jack was in his teens, we played ball outdoors nearly every weekend regardless of the weather. Jack is now grown, has two young children, a little gray hair and a job that frequently involves weekends, so it's not easy to disappear for two hours of basketball.

The two young men I didn't recognize have changed too. Skinny teenagers when I was on the court with them, they are now both married, fathers and probably in their mid 30s.

Except for a bigger belly, I haven't changed much since we played ball together. The white hair and glasses are the same, and, to everyone's disappointment, including my own, I'm using the same old one-liners. If my team is getting creamed, I say, "We'll get them on conditioning," (we never do) and, when one of my jump shots goes in the basket and then pops out, I say, with firm conviction, "There is no God."

My playing days must end sometime. Until then I'd like to ask a favor of those who remember me from way back. Say hello by all means, shake my hand, ask how Jack and I are doing and give me your name along with a couple of obvious clues. Something along the lines of: "Hi, Larry. How are you? How's your son? I'm Joe. We used to play every weekend over on Sunrise Highway. You chewed tobacco all the time, wore a real disgusting elbow brace and drove that ugly blue Chevette. My cousin, Steve, was usually with me. Big, tall, left-handed guy who was always blocking your shots. Good to see you."

And I will say, as I always do because it's true, "It's good to be seen at my age."

The Good News: *I have yet to get into the car and head for the park to play ball and stop half way there and wonder where the hell it was I was going.*

Enjoying Yourself, Living Or Dead, At A Memorial Service

Obituaries in the newspaper aren't nearly as boring as they used to be. Every few months I hear or read about the death of someone I worked with or went to school with. If I liked the person, there's usually an awkward half-hour struggle to eke out a few handwritten lines of condolence to his or her survivors.

Writing a eulogy for a sibling or a close friend is also difficult and delivering it at a funeral or memorial service is even harder. But you'll be glad you did later, at least that's been my experience.

A few weeks after my younger brother, Dwight, died, Irene and I went to Sarasota, Florida, for a memorial service. Dwight was an accountant, a man who paid attention to details, and that included what he wanted to happen at his memorial service. Too bad he couldn't have been there. I think he would have liked it.

I wrote him a letter about it. Never did mail it because I didn't know what address to use, and besides I didn't know how I would react if I sent it to "c/o Dwight K. McCoy, In Heaven," and it came back stamped, "Addressee Unknown." In case there's a bookstore wherever he is, maybe he'll see this and finally read his letter.

> Dear Dwight,
>   I'm not sure if they ever scattered you in the chapel courtyard as they were supposed to, but we held a memorial service a month after you died, pretty much following your instructions. I say 'pretty

much' because there were, as always, a few screw-ups. Some of them you would have enjoyed. One of them would have driven you crazy.

Let's do crazy first. They messed up your name. They used the wrong middle initial. On the programs you were Dwight A. McCoy, proving perhaps that the 1st Presbyterians of Sarasota are 2nd or 3rd in proofreading. Look at it this way: You were 'a' McCoy, just not Dwight A. McCoy. Maybe next time—do you know by now if there IS a next time?—you can supervise the printing of the programs.

You lucked out on the weather. We had non-stop heavy rain and lots of lightning, the perfect touch for a funeral or remembrance service. Dr. K. presided, as you requested, and was a terrific choice. He's warm, intelligent, down-to-earth, and he obviously liked you.

It's a pity your brothers and sister are such bad listeners. Before we went into the sanctuary, Dr. K. gave specific instructions that the family was to sit in the first row closest to the pulpit. We paraded in and proceeded to sit in the first row FARTHEST from the pulpit. What a bunch of losers. After glances from the good Dr., we three sheep rose and shuffled over to where we should have been in the first place.

Mrs. K. sang the song you wanted and was fine, but a lady who did 'For The Mountains Shall Depart' stole the show. She was dynamite. White hair with a strong voice, and when she finished she stood stone-still for five or ten seconds, adding to the power of her performance. I never did get her name, although I did compliment her afterwards.

The church big cheese—the good looking southern lady with the accent and the doctorate—got into the act, reading scripture in a way that made me think that before God got to her she probably wanted to be Holly Hunter.

I made a little speech and asked right off the bat whether anyone knew if Holly Hunter and Hunter S. Thompson were related. Just joking. Calm down. Actually I spent several minutes explaining that you never forgot anything, and why I found that so damn annoying. It wasn't normal for someone—YOU—to remember details about cars and apartments I had right after college when I'd forgotten all about them. You could name the make and year of every car you saw on the street and knew every flower, shrub, every actor and movie. How did you find the time for all this? Very, very annoying to those of us who ignore most of the things around us.

I did praise you, both your serious and funny side.

- (Serious) You always worried, despite all your own battles, that someone else might need your help, so you spent Thanksgiving and Christmas feeding others at support group dinners.
- (Funny) You were an Indiana wise guy until the end with your 'business' card ('Have The Best Day You Can') and your T-shirt ('I'm All Stressed Out And Have No One To Choke.')

While my comments weren't nearly as eloquent or as moving as you deserved, you would have appreciated my ox-like agility displayed on the way to and from the pulpit. A heavy metal sign with the word 'RESERVED' was on the railing of the pew where we were seated.

As I stood up, I grabbed the railing and the sign came off in my hand. Naturally I pretended nothing had happened while fumbling like mad to put it back. When I returned after my speech, the same thing happened. Your klutz of a brother was a perfect 2 for 2 for the day.

The reception was held in the hall next door, and we took your advice on ordering food from the Publix supermarket. You can stop worrying. No one left hungry, and what I had, following several long conversations with some of your friends and some hugging and crying among ourselves, was quite good.

After thanking the church ladies for their help, we headed back to your place to clean things up a bit and throw some stuff away. Wish you could have been there with me when I walked in. Your oldest brother and your only brother-in-law were working in the kitchen and had on bright latex gloves. You would have had a better line, but I asked if they were on their way to a urologists' convention.

That evening we had dinner at the Thai place you liked and reminisced about you, the folks and growing up. It was a good meal and a good time. The next morning we all got on planes and went home.

Not long afterwards a bill arrived from the funeral home that picked you up from the hospice and made sure you were cremated. Mind if I ask what kind of deal the family master accountant worked out with these folks? The bill was for $6. As I've told you a hundred times, it was so frustrating (here we go again) to grow up with a younger brother who always had money while his older, and

*presumably wiser, brother never had any. I'll bet you
got a little bit of cash on you right now, don't you.
Next time we see each other you can spring for the
Bloomin' Onion at the Outback. I hope it's not too
hot for onions where you are.
Love,
Larry*

The Good News: *If the person you eulogize
doesn't like what you said about him, there really isn't
much he can do about it, is there?*

Me And Rodney Yee

In my mid-60s, a doctor told me I had a nerve rubbing a disc, or perhaps it was the other way around, and I looked for ways to eliminate the tingling I had in my lower back every morning. Yoga, something I knew nothing about, came to mind after reading a piece in *The Wall Street Journal* about aging would-be athletes who had taken it up, hoping it would allow them to still play their favorite sport without causing further injury or damage.

I went to a bookstore and bought, as usual, the first thing I saw. It was *Moving Toward Balance, 8 Weeks of Yoga With Rodney Yee*. I brought it home, and both Julie and Deena, my daughter-in-law, complimented me. "Rodney Yee. Very good." He is apparently fairly well known. Reading the book, I found this on page 37, under version two of Downward-Facing Dog Pose:

> As you feel the tip of your tailbone curling forward, deepen your groins by allowing your groins to drop toward your sacrum and sitting bones.

Excuse me. I'm a transplanted Hoosier, grandson of a farmer, son of a salesman, first in the family to graduate from college, but am I missing a part? Do most people have "groins?" If you saw me on the street, could you tell that I'm one or two "groins" short? Or do only Asian people have "groins?" I've been to all sorts of doctors and been shot, thumped, pinched, twisted, pulled and rubber-fingered and not a one of them ever suggested I wasn't all there, body-wise. If Rodney Yee knows what he's talking about, that could explain why I was cut from the high school basketball team. All the other guys had "groins." I didn't. I always thought the reason I was kicked off the team was because I was terrible. That and the fact I couldn't see 15 feet ahead of me without my glasses and stupid vanity kept me from wearing them on the court. But like everything else at 70 plus, it's getting pretty damn late for a do-over.

The Good News: *With or without the proper number of "groins," anyone doing the Downward-Facing Dog Pose looks pretty silly. Arf, arf!*

The Secret To Night Driving

Among the things I know I don't do as well as I used to is driving at night. I'm not as confident, don't feel as in control as I once did. I wear glasses all the time and see fine. In the daytime. At night though, when I'm behind the wheel, I have a major problem with the headlights on other cars. They're all too damn bright for these aging eyes. Flipping down that lever on the rearview mirror doesn't help much. Yes, it cuts down on the glare but distorts the hell out of how close the car behind you is.

It always seems that whenever I'm on a major road after dark some moron with bright lights (it's actually his car that has the piercing, bright lights; the moron himself is very dim of bulb) is six inches behind me going 60+ miles an hour while heading toward me is his cousin, another moron, who has installed klieg lights in his car. Blue klieg lights. When this happens, I can't see a blessed thing, and I frantically try to remember all the words to "What A Friend We Have In Jesus."

Although everyone else's lights are too bright, mine aren't bright enough. Not too long ago Irene and I were driving home on a busy parkway after an evening with friends, and I flashed on my brights, hoping that would help me see the faint lines in the road. My normal headlights were so weak, or so it seemed, that I wasn't sure they were on. They were, but I wanted something stronger.

It was also raining at the time. Not a downpour, yet steady enough to wobble the needle on my confidence meter. After about 20 minutes, my hands began to hurt, and I quickly realized why: I was choking the steering wheel as if

I were on the world's scariest roller coaster and didn't dare relax. (If a steering wheel had lungs, mine would have been coughing.)

The most exciting night driving experience is when you see things in the road and step on the brakes or slam them on, only to discover what you thought looked like an evergreen tree standing upright in your lane was either simply a shadow or absolutely nothing. Startled by the sharp brake action, Irene, or whoever is with me, will shout, "What are you doing?" Or "What's wrong?" I believe that a firm "nothing" is a much better answer than, "Well, you know I thought I saw an evergreen tree growing in the middle of the road and put on the brakes, so I wouldn't run into it. Don't tell me you didn't see it."

This exhilarating illusion occurs most often on my way home from skiing in the Catskills. It's a three-hour drive each way and that, along with four hours or more of skiing, makes it a long day. My normal routine is to stop a short distance from the slopes for a potty break and to fuel up the car and myself. I buy a large black coffee and at least one candy bar, trying to pace things so there is still some coffee and a square or two of chocolate left in case an entire evergreen forest suddenly pops up in front of me. (ATTENTION: New York State Department of Motor Vehicles. I'm only joking, for the most part anyway. Have a nice day.)

I don't, thank heavens, see evergreens on the road during the day, but about two years ago my son decided that regardless of the hour, if he were traveling with me, he was going to drive. It's fair to say, I think, Jack believes I don't put nearly enough pedal to the metal.

When I'm by myself at night on a drive of some distance, I have the radio on fairly loud, or, if I'm in Irene's Volvo, I'm playing a CD, probably the same two cuts over and over for miles and singing and "humbling"—a combination of humming and mumbling—along with the music.

As for the secret to driving at night, sorry, but I don't think there is a secret. Prayer might be one approach to try. To those who don't pray regularly and still want to venture out in the car at night, all I can say is suck it up and good luck! Oh, and watch it with the bright lights and stay the hell out of my way.

The Good News: *Driving home in the dark from skiing, I have yet to see, standing in the middle of the road, the Mormon Tabernacle Choir.*

I Don't Shop At A Store Whose Name I Can't Pronounce

I hate Christmas shopping more and more every year. The fact that I'm on a fixed income has nothing to do with it. I try to be generous at Christmas and hope America's retailers have one heck of a holiday season, but I get more frustrated every December because I don't know any of the stores these days.

Rachel's Christmas list one year included a gift certificate from Hollister. What is that I wondered? Is Hollister's full name International Hollister? Could it be the remnants from various mergers of the old International Harvester, the people who make tractors? Rachel wants a gift certificate for a tractor? Is it possible that she wants to plant corn so she can distill a batch of bourbon a few years from now for Grandpa? Go, Girl, go.

A mall on Long Island where I go—almost always because I desperately need something and am confident it will take me all of three minutes to buy it—is loaded with places I've never heard of. One of them is L'Occitane. I looked them up on the Internet and found: "L'Occitane shares the colors, scents and traditions of the south of France with the world." I take this to mean that L'Occitane would be the perfect spot to zip into if you had a hankering for some crusty bread, wine, a pack of Gitanes and perhaps 40 or more snide comments about U.S. foreign policy over the last half century.

When I was a kid, Sears Roebuck and Montgomery Ward were two of the best stores around. They not only sold good stuff, you didn't have to think twice about how to say their names. At the mall I go to there is Geox, Jurlique and bebe. There is also something called Guess. They don't know? I'm supposed to guess what they have?

Even the stores I'm familiar with are selling things I've never heard of. At Lord & Taylor—killing time while Irene pursued her long-time hobby of touching every single piece of women's clothing on display—there was a sign in the men's department for "wool novelty pants." Within the bounds of decency, may I ask what is the novelty? Is it hidden in the pants somewhere? A mini cell phone? A yo-yo? A little plastic car? Presuming someone buys these things, are you expected to say something to your wife or partner when you put them on for a night out? "Hey, Babe," (repeated lifting of the eyebrows here) "I'm wearing my novelty pants." As you can tell, I haven't a clue. They looked like plain old chinos to me.

Rachel got her wish, as many granddaughters do when dealing with grandpas, but just barely. After looking at the mall map, I made several fruitless laps around two floors searching for a store with a big Hollister sign out front. Nothing. I seemed to always end up outside this very dark facade that looked like a Chinese restaurant but had no noticeable markings. I was about to give up when I spotted a small, discreet Hollister logo by the "restaurant." In I went. Although it was mid-December, every young female thing working behind the counter had a bare belly. Loud music was playing. It didn't look like a place selling real clothes. I didn't roam around much beyond the checkout counter area, but the things I did see for sale appeared to be thin, tight rags, expensive thin, tight rags. One of the belly dancers swiped my Amex card, I signed and I was out of there. At least I can pronounce "Hollister." What must it be like in those places with the, to me, unpronounceable names? Neither I nor my American Express card really wants to know.

The Good News: *Rachel now favors American Eagle, a well-lit store with stuff that resembles real clothing. Imagine that.*

A Thank You To The U.S. Government And American Taxpayers

When my first Social Security check was deposited in the bank, I was still working full-time, and it took me a while to get over feeling guilty about taking the money. At age 65 and in good health, I knew there were people who needed it more than I did. Following a bit of mental wrestling, I realized, Hey, Dummy, you paid into Social Security for more than 50 years. Take the money and relax.

I would like, however, to thank the U.S. Government and the American taxpayers for their previous help. The taxpayers are to be thanked for the salary and free housing during the ten years my family of four lived in West Germany where I worked for Radio Free Europe. We really appreciated the air fare every other year for home leave, which enabled us to see our parents and grandparents and provided a little extra boost to the U.S. economic indicators for August with our frenzied visits to Sears, Macy's and many Dairy Queens.

All those years of airline tickets, paychecks and housing added up to serious money, but your best investment came more than half a century ago and didn't set you back much at all. A pair of ordinary, brown shoes issued when I signed up for ROTC at Indiana University.

Mr. and Mrs. Taxpayer, I wore your shoes to work four nights a week, stocking shelves at the A&P. You squat a lot stocking shelves, and as the weeks went by the toes of the shoes began to curl like the ends of a pagoda roof. Then one chilly morning, there was an inspection of ROTC freshmen in full uniform. When the inspector got to me, he took one look and barked, "What happened to your shoes?"

"I wear them to work at the A&P, SIR."

This snappy, factual answer apparently wasn't covered in the training manuals for the Reserve Officers' Training Corps. After glaring at me for what seemed like five minutes, the inspector uttered the complete name and middle initial of a major religious figure and moved on. (This may have been the same day I stumbled trying to get back into formation, lugging an empty ROTC rifle. To keep from falling, I instinctively used the rifle to regain my balance and jammed the barrel straight into the wet ground. I think the formation was dismissed before I dug even half of the mud out of the barrel. The ROTC folks were smart; you got to take their shoes home but not their weapons.)

Those shoes furnished by U.S. taxpayers lasted well into my junior year. Because of your generosity, I was able to earn money for college and beers and to learn:

(a) Too much squatting isn't good for you or your shoes.
(b) Curled shoes perplex uniformed superiors.
(c) I would make a terrible soldier.
(d) And the most practical lesson, which has been passed on to all my kids and grandkids: if you drop a glass jar of beets or applesauce at the supermarket or at home, stick your foot out right away. You can frequently break the fall enough that the glass doesn't shatter when it hits the floor.

All-in-all that's a pretty impressive return on a mere $20 investment in shoes. I can only hope you are getting your money's worth this time around with that part of your

Social Security deductions that goes into my bank account.
I'm pumping every dime of that money right back into the
economy as fast as I can. If you don't believe me, ask Irene.

The Good News: *I don't have to squat anymore,
and yet I still get a check every month. What a country.*

"Sure. Go Swimming If You Want."

If you like to keep active, there's one thing you can count on when you go to the doctor regardless of what's wrong with you. He'll tell you it's okay to go swimming. Your arm could be dangling limply at your side after a bad fall in the shower or you twisted a knee so badly you can't bend it without excruciating pain, and you'll still hear, "Sure. Go swimming if you want." Why they say this I don't know but let's try a little experiment. Column A is for you to list a few of the doctors you can remember seeing over the past 20 years. Column B is for the doctors you have seen swimming over the past 20 years. My own list follows:

COLUMN A   COLUMN B

Dr. H (A real rude dude)*   . . . .
Dr. B (World's slowest biller)   . . . .
Dr. Sh (Thorough but slow)*   . . . .
Dr. G (The best there is)   . . . .
Dr. Sa (Good sense of humor)** . . . .
Dr. E (Tells good stories)   . . . .
Dr. D (Looks like Rock Hudson) . . . .
Dr. I (Needs new shirts)   . . . .

* Irene thinks these two are idiots.
** Used to say "wonder what that could be" and then look in a medical book while you were on the examining table.

I could go on and on listing other doctors and Column

B would still be blank. Yeah, some of these guys may belong to posh country clubs that don't let in the likes of me. But I've stayed at a few fancy spots with magnificent pools, and I haven't seen any of them swimming there either.

When I was in my 60s, a problem with one of my knees flared up again and naturally the suggestion was that I try swimming for exercise. Rachel, my oldest granddaughter who loves to swim, started going with me to an indoor pool every weekend. When my knees were okay, I could play basketball for two hours with no problem, but after half an hour of swimming—sore knee or no sore knee—I was pooped.

Rachel and I frequently shared part of the pool with a woman who looked to be in her 50s, wore what resembled a cover for a Mixmaster on her head and never stopped moving or grunting. She did a sort of modified dog paddle and made "uhn-uhn-uhn" noises at regular intervals. The lady was in the water before we got there and after we left and never stopped. It wasn't really swimming, just treading water, so it didn't bother me that she had a hell of a lot more stamina in the water than I had.

One day when I had been in the pool by myself for about 15 minutes, an older woman I had never seen before asked if she could share a lane with me. I said, "Of course." She must have been 80, both in years and weight, and could only be objectively described as wizened or even post-wizened.

She asked if I preferred one side of the lane over the other, and I said, "No." She climbed in and started swimming. Real swimming, no sissy dog paddling. Arms and legs smoothly cutting through the water. Length after length without stopping. I would do a length, occasionally two, and stop to catch my breath and to reflect on how exhausted I was.

I was in the water for maybe another 20 minutes,

sharing the lane with her. She never stopped. Not once. She was still at it when I got out. And she wasn't making a sound, not a peep. This was easy, a breeze. For her. Me? I felt awful. Humiliated.

Irene had gone with me that day—she used the exercise room—and, as we drove to lunch, I told her about this shriveled Esther Williams. I ordered an ice tea with my meal when what I really wanted was a double bourbon and a barrel of sympathy. I got neither. Irene didn't think it was that big a deal.

This is the sort of thing you probably need to discuss with a professional—a shrink. I haven't seen any of them in the pool either. Have you?

The Good News: *With all the rolls around my belly, I certainly don't like the way I look in a bathing suit, so no one would think of ever describing me as "wizened."*

Weathering The Next Economic Storm

During the 2008 economic meltdown, we did what all sane people did. Panicked! After weeks of watching our investments shrivel, I sent an email to Bif, our financial planner at one of America's top banks:

Several times a day we wonder, are we going to lose every penny we have invested?

He responded instantly: "Yes."

That's not funny, but I am kidding. Bif didn't reply to my email. He's not allowed to. I didn't know that. I also didn't know I wasn't supposed to send him emails. There is a higher authority at the bank that intercepts such communications. The good-natured explanation given me was that the bank didn't want customers firing off emails to its investment personnel asking that 5,000 shares of Uncle Ralph's Barely Drinkable Vodka be bought or sold. The message might not be seen right away, leaving the customer unhappy that the instructions weren't carried out immediately. The financial planner could be in a meeting, at lunch, on the phone, on vacation or over at the Hampton Inn sipping some of Uncle Ralph's Barely Drinkable Vodka with Lillian, the new teller.

As I understand it, business is to be done only in person or in "live" telephone conversations. Fair enough. I learned all this in Bif's office the day after I sent the email. To my surprise, Bif and his assistant, Roy Boy, said there hadn't been lots of people coming in to talk over concerns about their investments. They assured me, as they always do, that the stock market would rebound, that it had traditionally produced a solid rate of return over the long haul, that we had a good mix of stocks and bonds, and that it wouldn't be smart to pull out a big chunk of money because we would be locking in for good the losses we had so far suffered only on paper.

While all that made sense and was temporarily soothing, it didn't eliminate all our worries. Yes, we had lost money. No, we weren't in danger of going bankrupt or losing our house, but there are many hours in the day, many chances to fret about the damage being done to your nest egg. Working on the assumption that Bif and Roy Boy didn't want to have a hand-holding session with me every other day, I devised my own list of home remedies to keep my mind off the stock market and finances. The next time the economy hits a rough patch you might want to try a couple of these.

- Make a list of all the girls you kissed in high school and where you kissed them. Not parts of their body, you pervert, but where—a park bench, a sofa, the kitchen, a car, the porch.
- Take a corkscrew and jab it into that web of skin between your thumb and index finger and twist as hard as you can. Do you really care now that the Dow is down 450 points? I didn't think so.
- Save a little money and go Green at the same time. When you were a kid you probably took a bath twice a week. Be a kid again. Shower or bathe only on Wednesday and Saturday. Should someone at the 7-Eleven say "You stink"—be a kid again—say "So does your mother" then run like hell.
- Put Bactine and a Band-Aid on that web of skin between your thumb and index finger.
- With the market numbers so bad you don't dare look at them, this would be an ideal time to focus

on your hammer toes. Remove shoes and socks and then grab the largest dictionary you own and drop it squarely on the hammer toes. You can't tell me that doesn't take your mind off your portfolio. Repeat as necessary.

- Switch to a cheaper brand of your favorite nighttime medication, be it Scotch, vodka, gin, bourbon, rum, but by all means don't forget to take it. If you can't remember whether you took your evening medication, don't jeopardize your health—have another dose. Or two or . . . .
- Get a copy of *It's A Wonderful Life* and play it over and over.
- Crawl into bed and eat, all by yourself, an entire package of Double Stuf Oreos. Repeat as necessary.
- Dig out your Monopoly set and challenge your wife and dinner guests to a game for old times' sake. Insist on being the banker and slip yourself $200 every time any one lands on Chance or Community Chest. Feels good to have a little extra cash on hand, doesn't it.
- Think back to your worst boss. Write his or her name on a piece of cardboard and pin or nail it to a tree. Using a baseball bat or a 2x4, pound the cardboard to smithereens. Get another piece of cardboard and do it again. And again. Pretty dumb, yes, but you can burn up a solid half an hour without turning on the TV or the computer to check how the market is doing or undoing.

The Good News: *Although bankers are an easy target for ridicule, our guys, Bif and Roy Boy, have great senses of humor. At least I think they do.*

Say What's On Your Mind; Put It On Your Chest

You don't have to try to impress anyone these days, so you can do whatever the hell you want or don't want whenever the hell you want or don't want. Don't feel like shaving today? Don't. In no mood to put on a clean shirt? Then don't. No one, except maybe your wife, will know that you've worn the same shirt for three long days. And with the laundry hamper only half full, it makes no sense to waste water, soap and electricity. This means you can get at least another day or two out of the underwear you put on last Thursday. Or was it a week ago Thursday? You're not going to the movies, you don't have opera tickets, so why bother?

This new relaxed attitude about your wardrobe opens the way for made-to-order T-shirts with silly sayings on them. Why not? Don't tell me you have never stood in front of a store window and laughed at what's written on some of the T-shirts, especially the dirty ones. You don't have to get down in the gutter to have some fun on your chest.

Here are a few ideas I've thought about asking a store to put on T-shirts for me.

"When I was your age, I didn't think I would end up looking like this either."

"Kiss me. I'm harmless. Nothing works. Not even Viagra."

"I tried to donate this for medical research but got rejected."

"So what if I was a lousy father? I'm a hell of a grandpa."

"You think this is ugly. You should see my brother."

"I used to be as smart as you think you are."

"Yep. This is what you have to look forward to."

"Out of my way. I'm late for my depression class."

"As you can see, I've enjoyed myself."

"Dr. Kevorkian was in jail the day I really needed him."

"Thanks for your Social Security payments. If you're ever in Florida, look us up."

"Is this what they mean when they talk about 'BULKING UP?' "

"If you're gonna whine, don't waste my time."

If you look good in a T-shirt, save your money. These would look best on those of us with generous lumps and humps. We've worked hard for them and might as well get some mileage out of them.

The Good News: *Wear any of the above on your chest and your dining out expenses will be drastically slashed. No one in the family will want to be seen in public with you.*

Making Those All Important Final Arrangements

Even if you're in terrific shape and look years younger (you think) than 70, the kids are asking questions about what they should do with your body when you're done with it. You're also being teased more than usual about how much money you've spent recently on new skis and long trips. Slackers that we are, Irene and I had a will drawn up 10 years ago and have done nothing since. No arrangements have been made for burial or cremation. The two of us have had brief conversations about what each wants done, but they usually end with my making a bad joke.

Both Julie and Jack say I'm good at changing the subject when things get serious. I don't know where they got that idea. Maybe they jumped to that conclusion after I warned Irene that if she dies before I do her tombstone will say: "She Wasn't Always Too Tired."

Irene can be just as flippant. When Jack asked, "What do you want for your fiftieth?" (anniversary), she said, "To be able to stand up." Now there's an achievable goal for you.

It is time, I suppose, to take action if you've piddled. Our kids certainly know where we bank and that most of what we have is there. Whether they have any clue how much there is, I'm not sure. They've heard us say that Bif and Roy Boy, our bankers, have told us we have enough money to live to age 99, and we have threatened to see if we can prove them right. (Jack, by the way, calls Bif and Roy Boy "the luggage kings" because he's always joking that when he goes to the bank he sees them with new suitcases in their offices, about to skip town with scads of money.)

One of these days fairly soon Irene and I need to put on our straight faces and sit down with the kids and have a heart-to-heart. I imagine it going something like this:

Me: "Well, we're obviously getting up there, and your mother and I thought it was time we got serious and had this little talk. Sooo. You ought to know that if we both keeled over tomorrow there would be about 17 to 18 million dollars in various funds at the bank. Pretty good, huh?"

(I pause here so the kids can gasp and Irene can start yelling, "Larry! What are you talking about? Come on! Don't believe a word he's saying." After some hubbub, I continue.)

Me: "Well, lighten up. That was a small joke, wasn't it. I didn't actually say the 17 to 18 million was in OUR account. We don't have anywhere near that much. In fact we don't have a God damn cent except for some measly Savings Bonds. Sorry, Guys. We spent it all. Vacations in Hilton Head, Austria, the Finger Lakes. Plane tickets. New skis. The White Barn Inn in Kennebunkport, Gramercy Tavern in Manhattan. It all adds up. As I say, we're sorry. That about wraps it up. Who wants a drink?"

(At this point, if not sooner, Irene will undoubtedly take charge, apologize and complain over and over, "You promised you were going to be serious!" I will snicker, my specialty, and she will hint at a ballpark number for what we do have in the bank and tell them about the will and how everything is to be split equally. She will remind them that the same goes for the house, and either she or perhaps one of the kids will toss out a figure on what the place should sell for. After Julie and Jack and Lynn and Deena have asked any questions, all presumably answered straight by Irene, we move on to an entertaining discussion of last rites.)

Me: "Okay, now that the dirty business of money is out of the way, it's my turn again. Let's talk about what we want to happen after we're gone. Your mother wants to be cremated, at least that's what she said the last time we discussed it, which was two hours ago.

"You know me. I ain't very big on barbecues. I want to be buried. And in the casket with me I want you to throw in a bunch of those big rocks from the side of the driveway. As many as you can. Be quiet, Irene. Every time I stumble on one of those damn rocks around the flower beds you tell me to pick up my feet. It's a lot easier, Schatzi, if we pick up the rocks. Hush! You'll get your turn again.

"We've got an appointment next Wednesday to talk things over with the people at Pinelawn in Farmingdale. I think they do both cremations and burials. We'll make sure you get copies of anything we sign out there.

"Irene is going to say she doesn't want any kind of service or ceremony, but that's nonsense and we all know it. You'll do something for her if I'm not around. Shut up, Irene. I've got the floor.

"I don't really care whether or not you have some kind of small, private funeral for me, but I do want a memorial service. A month or two after I die. By the way, please tell people I 'died.'

Don't say that I 'passed.' Where the hell did that come from? It's bullshit. Everyone fails. No one 'passes.' So please.

"Now, the memorial service. You know all our friends. Invite them, of course, and the guys I played ball with all those years. Tom Foos and the others. Jack knows most of them. And notify the people who remember me from CBS and the RFE crew in Munich. You tell a couple and the word will quickly get out to the rest.

"The memorial service is meant to be a fun thing. No long, sad eulogies or people choking up. We want laughs, jokes, raunchy stuff. Listen up. I've got a short wish list. (1) Jack, see if you can use your photography and computer skills to phony up some good-sized picture of me in which I appear to have a woody. The picture would go up front near the speaker's stand. The news people I worked with will definitely be expecting something off-color and in bad taste. I can't let them down. Probably most of those who show up will be too busy worrying about how they look to notice I have my last woody, but those who do see it will laugh and say, 'That son-of-a-bitch. It's just like him.' (2) Julie, go through my CDs and pick out a country one to play while people come in and leave. Alan Jackson maybe. A lot of his songs are happy or as happy as country music gets. I love George Jones but not this time. He's the saddest-sounding fuck I've ever heard. Bad choice of words but it's true. (3) When things start to drag and no one else seems to want to get up and recount some outrageous thing I did or said, one of you—and I bet you flip a coin for this—has to stand up and read word for word that great piece of mine that all the ski magazines turned down, the one about farting in Austria. That should clear the hall real fast. I've already made copies of that literary masterpiece and attached them to the will. You'll be glad to hear there is no (4)."

I'll stop. Perhaps there's an idea or two back there that you might steal or modify for your own service. More likely you now have a much clearer fix on what you don't want to happen. In either case, it's time you got ready to face the music down the road. Cheer up. Even if we are "well past" our primes, at least we won't have to spend our Golden Years with another Clinton or another Bush in the White House. Thank you, Jesus!

The Good News: *Although few of us are geniuses, we've already lived twice as long as Mozart did. Plus we don't have to wear frilly shirts like he did.*

Two Codgers Humming

If you're like me, you have gone to the same barbershop for years, and you and the barbers have grown old together. It's only when you sit in the chair, though, that you get a full sense of how these old-timers are aging. The guy who frequently cuts my hair shuffles around the chair. I can't imagine how he gets across a busy street. He should leave Long Island immediately and move to Maine where drivers instantly hit the brakes when they see a pedestrian in a crosswalk a mile away.

It's not the shuffling that bothers me. It's the realization that he has a sharp instrument in his hand and electrical tools on the counter nearby, and the scissors and clippers are going to be very close to my eyes, ears, mouth, nose and neck for the next seven to eight minutes. Fortunately, I take my glasses off when I climb in the chair, so even if I looked down at his hands I wouldn't know for sure how close they were to jabbing me in the throat or whether they were shaking. I do see well enough without my specs to occasionally detect a Band-Aid on the barber's thumb or a finger. Spotting one of those is always comforting. How did he cut himself? Am I "next"?

This is indeed a barber shop, staffed by barbers with names like Joe and Arnie. These aren't stylists named Jason or Darien who spend five minutes massaging a green gel into your hair and another ten using a blow dryer on it. (Having never used a blow dryer or been to a stylist, I made up that last part. But based on my thorough research—strolls around town—all the stylists here look to be about 19 and have real bad haircuts with a slicked-down look as though someone poured a Starbucks mint mocha chip Frappuccino over their heads.)

Things are very simple where I go. The guys cut your hair, take the apron from around your neck, flip off the trimmings and put the apron back on before smearing lather around your ears to do your sideburns. Newspaper reporters like to idealize barber shops as key pillars of democracy where the pulse of American men can be detected in debates and discussions on hefty issues. There's little of that at my place, and for that I'm grateful. What I've never been crazy about is the oldies radio station they always have on. Every time I go for a haircut it seems Neil Diamond is singing "Sweet Caroline," and, as if that isn't bad enough, two codgers, either cutting hair or having theirs cut, are trying to hum along. It's brutal.

I really shouldn't complain. The barbers do a decent job, and you can walk in with only $20 in your pocket and leave, after paying and tipping, with a few bucks left over. Not enough for a Starbucks mint mocha chip Frappuccino mind you, but enough for a couple of $1 scratch off lottery tickets.

P.S. While we're talking oldies music, let me say that if PBS would promise never to air another doo wop program during its fund-raising drive, I would change my will to give them my house.

The Good News: *You'll never walk out of my barber shop looking like a TV anchor or an evangelist. And there's a lot to be said for that.*

A Home Entertainment Center In Your Mailbox

If you get all sorts of catalogs in the mail and throw nearly all of them away without even a glance, stop! You're missing out on a great form of cheap entertainment. I didn't realize this until I took a close look at a catalog from Orvis, the people in Vermont who sell the bare necessities to rich people. You know—cashmere baseball hats, driving shoes, walking sticks and therapeutic beds for older dogs.

Judging by a men's clothing catalog, Orvis likes its copywriters to have previous experience in teaching English As A Tenth Language. Under an ad for "Irish Setter Soft Paw Chukka," it is said, "Each detail adds to the comfort: supple full-grain leather, an oiled canvas collar fabric, moisture-wicking nylon lining, memory foam, an EVA midsole, and a TPU shank." (I would kill for TPU shank if only I knew what it was.) I take it these are for men and not dogs, an assumption based on the sizes listed. I can't remember the last time I saw an Irish setter wearing a 14 EE. It's also been a while since I overheard anyone say, "Hey, Wally, that sure is a sweet pair of chukkas you have on." They're boots and Orvis wants $119 for them. While that seems high, they do come with "memory foam," something that all of us over 70 really need.

Chukkas aren't the only fun things Orvis sells. Nearly every page brought a smile along with many questions.

Can the "Montana Morning Jacket" be worn on Long Island? If the answer is "yes," can it be worn at suppertime, which is pretty darn late in the evening much of the time?

One page showed a "Bison Money Belt." How long have bison had their own money? Is it stronger than the euro?

What is it you are supposed to do when wearing the "Escape Pants" on page 108? Is it possible to buy these if you are in prison?

Orvis offers its customers "Invincible Extra Socks." Do the U.S. Marines and Army Special Ops know about these? According to the catalog, the socks are "washable." What a great idea. What will these Orvis folks think of next?

Is the "Original Moleskin Vest" for sale or just for rent? Does it have a strange smell?

The "Waterproof Loden Wool Shooting Coat" looks handsome and solid, but it sounds dangerous. How much wool can a loden coat shoot? How far does it shoot the wool? What are the chances the wearer of this coat will be hit in the face by shot wool? That hurts, right?

Does the "Quick-Draw Cell Phone Holster" come with instructions? Does Orvis provide on-site classes on the use of holsters like it does for fly-fishing rods? Is there a money back guarantee if you're wearing a "Quick-Draw Cell Phone Holster" and still miss a call?

The "Original 'Ratcatcher' Moleskin Pants" don't appear to have any extra pockets, so if you're successful where do you put the rats?

A headline on page 54 stated, "They call it football weather for a reason." I hate to be dense but what is the reason?

There was a "Bush Shirt," which the catalog described as "midweight." It wasn't clear whether that was a reference to the material or a cheap political shot. The catalog claimed the "Bush Shirt" was built "to keep you dry and cool on your adventures." Haven't we had enough adventures for a while?

We also get catalogs from Macy's, Restoration Hardware, Best Buy, Dover Publications and others. One of these days I should flip through them to see if they are as entertaining as the Orvis catalog. I regret that I discovered this pleasure so late. If only I had known years ago that there was something called the "Transatlantic Zip-Neck Sweater," maybe I could have saved some money on plane tickets to Europe and back.

The Good News: *Laughing at the rich never gets old.*

"ASHLEY! ASHLEY!"

Since the whole family knows you have a lot of free time, you are asked to spend part of it helping out. You could be asked to take your pre-teen granddaughter to a basketball game, one in which she is playing. Mom and Dad are busy at work that day, and you are told the games usually last about an hour. That may be technically true, but it sure won't feel like an hour. It will seem longer than the Watergate hearings and the 2008 presidential campaign combined.

In the game I watched, the teams played two halves, one half had two quarters, the other only one. This may explain why few of us can immediately name this country's most famous mathematician.

For a while you might find what is happening on the court fascinating. I define "for a while" in this instance as about one minute and 15 seconds. The way the game is played is for everyone to stand around—both offense and defense—bunched together, almost scrum-like, including the person with the ball. She dribbles and dribbles and dribbles, usually in one spot but sometimes actually moves in the direction of her team's basket. But don't get your hopes up. She'll soon dribble back to where she started.

Dribbling is inherently a hypnotic activity. Those without the ball wave their arms and shout over and over the name of the dribbler. "Ashley, Ashley, Ashley!" Should Ashley pass the ball to another girl, say, Heather, she will dribble and dribble and dribble, amid screams of "Heather, Heather, Heather!" About the time you want to call your periodontist and ask if he can drill four holes in your jaw that afternoon without anesthetic, miraculously one of the girls will shoot the ball at the basket. Amazing, and it's still only the first half of the game.

Whoever is supervising all this will call occasional time outs, allowing the girls to troop over to the sidelines, looking exhausted (yelling wears you out) while taking long gulps from their water bottles. Dribbling and screaming will soon resume, and way, way before the first half is over you will suddenly wish you had a job to go to or fantasize about how much more stimulating it would be if a good friend took a golf club and smacked you across the back with it for 20 minutes. Perhaps a game involving a group of average 11-year-old boys is about the same. A real shit load of dribbling and traveling and yelling. I just happened to have witnessed the girls' version.

This strikes me as calisthenics with a ball. If exercise and fitness are the objectives here, then I'd suggest it would be a more efficient use of time if the supervisor simply told all the kids to do jumping jacks for half an hour while screaming each other's names. That way we could all get the hell out of there and go home or go see the periodontist.

The Good News: *No one has ever asked you to coach kids this age.*

Hot Dogs, Hot Dogs. Who Wants A Hot Dog?

At 70 you still have one thing in common with a teenager: There are certain things you pray no one finds out about. When you were 16, things happened that you didn't dare tell your parents about. Now you do things that your kids don't need to know, not right away anyway.

For instance. Jack invited us over for lunch and a swim one summer day. After phone calls and emails, it was established that lunch would be hot dogs on Jack's grill. He had the hot dogs. We had the buns. Irene and I put on our swimming suits, got in the car and headed for his house.

After a swim, lunch was mentioned. Irene said she packed hot dog buns plus some hamburger patties and hamburger buns. The problem was we couldn't find the bag she put them in. We looked around Jack's yard where we sat before climbing into the pool. I looked in his refrigerator. I looked in our car. No buns, no hamburger patties.

I made the short trip back home and looked all over the kitchen, the breakfast nook, the dining room. No buns, no hamburger patties. I called Irene, told her the news and said I would stop at a store on the way back.

This was all very bothersome because Irene and I were always looking for signs that we were losing it. Senior moments is the euphemism. Where was the damn bag? Then I remembered that before heading to Jack's I grabbed a bag off the kitchen counter and took it to the garbage can by the garage. Yes, indeed. It wasn't garbage after all. I opened the garbage can and there was the plastic bag, the handles tightly tied in knots. Inside, the hamburger and hot dog buns were snugly wrapped in their original plastic, the hamburger patties still encased in the package from the supermarket. And, best of all, the bag wasn't wet.

On the drive back to Jack's, I took everything out of the bag to double-check. I could see nothing— no moisture, no bugs—and could feel nothing. For lunch that day, Jack, Irene and Larry McCoy all had one hot dog and one cheeseburger, the buns as well as the burgers retrieved from a garbage can.

When Jack asked where I found the bag, I said it was in our driveway near plants Irene had fussed with before we came over, an accurate, although incomplete explanation. "Garbage can" never was part of our conversation. It would be a better story, I suppose, if we had never told the truth. We did. Months later. If you remember back to your teens, it was hard then, too, to keep a secret for very long.

The Good News: *The cats in our neighborhood are a lazy bunch.*

A Stress Test Is One Thing, Waiting On The Results Another

More than a year before I retired I had a chest pain early one morning and woke up Irene to tell her and to ask her to get me some aspirin, which you're supposed to take if you think you might be having a heart attack. I took two aspirins, and we talked about driving to the hospital, calling 911 or trying to go back to sleep. We decided on the latter but when morning came I made an appointment with my doctor.

After an examination that included an EKG and a blood sample, the doctor said he wanted me to go for a stress test. I had never had one. Irene had, before her knee replacement operations. (One of her tests was scheduled on a day we planned to go to a concert, and, when I called a friend to offer her the tickets and explained why, she said, "A stress test? You're not enough?" Drum roll, please.)

My stress test was set for a Sunday morning (yes, Sunday). I had been instructed to cut out all caffeine at least 24 hours before and show up without breakfast. After completing lots of paper work, a lady named Kathy asked me some questions before sticking a needle in my arm. Next a male technician came in and inserted fluid into the needle. He told me to go have breakfast—"Eat something with fat in it, a burger or eggs, and drink 24 ounces of juice or cola"—and come back in an hour. I went home, scrambled two eggs, ate three chunks of cheddar cheese and two pieces of toast with honey and drank 24 ounces of cranberry juice. That's a lot of juice to get down in a short time.

After eliminating some of the liquid, I drove back to

the stress factory. The technician who shot me up with fluids put me on one of those very narrow tables all medical places love to see if you can center your big ass on. He said he needed me to hold my hands over my head and not move for 12 minutes while the machine took pictures of my heart. Twelve minutes? One quarter of playing time in the NBA. Not a problem. Why does every part of your body develop a desperate need for a good scratching whenever you're asked to assume a very uncomfortable position and hold dead-still?

I managed to do as told, and, when the machine stopped making funny noises, I went next door where an Asian lady doctor (a double minority working on Sunday) introduced herself and pointed to a treadmill. I got on and Kathy took my blood pressure three or four times while I worked the treadmill. When that was over, Kathy told me one of the doctors would call the next day to tell me the results. I said, "I'll take that bet." She insisted they were very good about calling right away.

Next stop was back to the waiting room. More heart pictures would be taken, post-exercising. The technician led me away again, and again it was 12 minutes with the hands over the head while lying motionless. When this session ended, he asked me to stay on the table while he checked his images. On his return, he said he didn't like some of the pictures. This was the point where our relationship soured, and I began to wonder if some form of waterboarding might be next.

I was told to hold my hands over my head for yet another 12 minutes. Oh, good. We're playing overtime today. "The images aren't clear," he explained. I knew instantly, of course, that he had seen something, something bad, very, very bad. I had a blocked artery, a deviated valve, a collapsed heart, a frog in my throat. Some God awful condition. Swallowing hard, it was hands over the head again and tick,

tick, tick-12 minutes finally pass. Wait a minute, he said. He had to check things. This time he was satisfied and said I could go.

While I was waiting for the elevator, the Asian lady doctor walked by and headed for the stairs. Of course, she had a strong, solid heart and took the four flights of stairs down. She didn't have a blocked artery, a deviated valve and all that. She got into her Mercedes and drove off. After my elevator ride, I crawled into my smaller version of a Mercedes, commonly known as a Volkswagen, and headed home.

The next day I went to work, knowing that both the heart doctor and the doctor who sent me for the stress test had my work and home phone numbers. I worked. I waited. Nothing. I knew they wouldn't call. I finished work, got the usual 8:06 train home and called Irene, as I always did, to tell her I was on it. For some reason she chatted and chatted. She's not a chatterer, but she was sure chattering that night, and I pretended to listen. Just chatter. No news. So I asked, "Any messages?"

"Oh, yes. I forgot to mention. The heart guy called, said your heart is good." Had the two of us been in the same room at that moment, I would have placed my hands firmly around her throat. When I got home, instead of two aspirins, I took two large bourbons, blocked artery, deviated valve, collapsed heart be damned.

The Good News: *You don't need a prescription for either aspirin or bourbon, and they both work wonders in their own ways.*

Bad Grandpa. He Shouldn't Have Said That.

One of the overlooked blessings of having grandkids is that they help clean up the language of grandfathers who spend way too much fucking time watching sports on television. Some guys have a bad habit of trying to find something dirty in the most innocent of things. Say the language of a play-by-play announcer. "Penetration," a word used frequently during NBA broadcasts when a player has driven close to the basket, always sends me into a juvenile state so deep that I repeat the word in a loud voice and twist its meaning.

As long as it's just you and a two-year-old in front of the set, you can get away with this. Once they get to be three or four you have to watch it. By then they are sponges and may well recite anything you say word for word to Grandma or Mommy and Daddy. You don't want your sweet little granddaughter saying, "Look at THOSE!" every time the camera shows a cheerleader. At least I hope you don't. Nor, after you are long gone, do you want all the grandkids to feel obligated, after they hear an ice cream truck passing through the neighborhood, to shout, "How would YOU like to go through life being called Mr. Softee?"

This self-censorship around the little ones means some of your oldest (and worst) lines are put on the DL (the Disabled List), a development certainly welcomed by a weary wife. When her steak arrives in a restaurant and she automatically says, "I didn't think it would be this big," you bite your lip, take a long drink of water or pat the shoulder of the nearest grandchild. You do not immediately bellow, "I'll bet you tell all the boys that."

You also have to be careful when Grandma is reading a book to an impressionable grandchild to not chime in with uninvited comment or analysis as the tale unfolds. This isn't cable television where almost anything goes. This is your living room, and the tiny, innocent thing on Grandma's lap has the prettiest smile.

My very filthy mind went full speed ahead when Irene read out loud the favorite book of one of our granddaughters, *Five Little Monkeys Bake A Birthday Cake*. First off the title should be changed to *Five Dumb Little Monkeys*. The monkeys decide to bake a cake for their mother's birthday but make a mess of things, and the fire department shows up when smoke fills the kitchen. We then learn it isn't their mother's birthday. Mama monkey, who is still in bed until the very end of the book, explains her birthday is the following day, pleasing the daylights out of the five dummies. Fine, they say, we'll bake another cake tomorrow. There is nothing to indicate these five will be smarter in 24 hours and do a better job than they did the first time when the fire department showed up.

There is no mention, the best I can recall, of a Dada monkey. The final page shows two firemen, their work done, sitting at the kitchen table eating burnt cake buried under frosting. They look very relaxed, not about to leave. In fact they look settled in. For the night. I should look in the bookstore one of these days to see if there is a sequel entitled *Six Little Monkeys And Daddy, The Fireman*.

The Good News: *Children's books are still being written, and grandparents are still reading them out loud to kids, even though they sometimes shorten the dickens out of them.*

My Very Own Sports Center Highlights

The day before he turned 60, Billy Crystal had what he called "the greatest moment of my life," taking a turn at bat with the New York Yankees in a spring training game. Video of the actor-comedian fouling a pitch off before striking out was splashed all over television and the Internet.

While I'd sure like to have a chance to bat for the Yankees, I wouldn't want ESPN or anyone else taking pictures. Billy Crystal didn't look ridiculous standing up there at the plate, but I would. Despite being a would-be jock all my life, I would embarrass myself, adding another highlight to a reel that keeps running through my head.

The reel begins in grade school at a big track meet held at the high school football stadium. The Kyger Grade School relay team—my team—was ahead when I got the baton. I took two steps before someone screamed, "You're going the wrong way." I stopped and, yes, started running the other way, the wrong way. The scream had to be the work of some high school smart ass. I wonder if that son of a bitch remembers that day as vividly as I do.

Years later on the same field as a sophomore on the football team, I was sent in during the first game of the season. The opposing team's best running back soon had the ball, and I raced toward him. Instead of making a tackle, I tried something different. I ran into him, standing straight up and going full speed. He bounced right up after a gain of 15 yards. I didn't get up because I was never getting up. It was my only play of the game.

We fast-forward 22 years. I'm a father with an eight-year-old son who has heard me talk of playing baseball all summer long as a kid. We are standing in the outfield when a ball is hit my way. Jack is excited. "Catch it, Daddy, catch it." He would have been so impressed if only I had. Or even came close. The ball that seemed such an easy chance dropped 30 feet from me.

There are tennis highlights too. The focus here is more on snazzy apparel than the caliber of play. While living in Munich, Germany, I occasionally swung a racket on classy clay courts where the players included the police chief and the goalie for the Bayern Munich soccer team. They and everyone else were in tennis whites. I wore blue Bermuda shorts, a ratty polo shirt and high-top Chucky Taylor basketball shoes. The club manager suggested to a German friend that I get with it.

Clothes are to blame for two other highlights. Wearing slick ski pants—"slick" as in slippery not chic—on a slope near Innsbruck, Austria, I fell and went sailing, head first, down the mountain. That sort of terrifying slide usually messes up your confidence. For two years or more. I didn't want to look like a sissy in front of my buddy who was a much better skier, so I assured him I could do this run and got back on the lift. Should this next highlight look like a replay, it isn't. I fell again, slid again, etc.

Basketball, my first love, takes up the bulk of the reel. There are scenes of my spraining ankles, pulling a hamstring, tearing a tendon in the arm, jamming fingers, getting my glasses broken, bleeding above the eye, playing in rain and snow, and even a glimpse of jump shots swishing the net.

Then there is the umbrella scene, one of the more recent and by far my most appalling "athletic" experience. At my age you don't move as well as you once thought you did nor do you try things that once were so easy. In the old days if I was shooting hoops alone outdoors and the ball got stuck between the backboard and the rim, a garbage can at the side of the court was turned over and climbed on to retrieve the ball.

I have stopped doing that. The jump down rattles the knees. Not long ago I encountered the stuck ball syndrome and took off a sneaker to throw at the ball. After several unsuccessful attempts, I heard a voice. A lady in the parking lot, holding an unopened umbrella, said, "I wondered what you were doing. Then I saw the ball."

Put the reel in Slo Mo for a truly awesome action shot. I walk over, take the lady's green umbrella, go back and poke the ball loose. Returning the umbrella, I thank her and sadly say, "I used to be able to get those," without further humiliating myself by explaining the now-discarded garbage can technique.

Before accepting the lady's umbrella, I had looked her over real good to make sure she didn't have a camera or one of those new phones that takes pictures. I didn't want anyone to see the real thing. The version being stored in my head was painful enough.

The Good News: *The nice umbrella lady hasn't come around asking for $300 to destroy the pictures she secretly took. Not so far.*

Being Picked On By An 18-Year-Old

That you are considered a numbskull is never more obvious than when you are traveling with an 18-year-old. This can really hurt if the one holding that opinion is your first grandchild. Yep, that one. The one you spent all those hours with, teaching him how to ride a bike, how to play baseball, basketball and Ping-Pong, the one you took on ski trip after ski trip, to little places and big.

And that's not all. Only a few years ago the kid now classifying you as a Nincompoop, Senior Grade begged you to take him out to an empty parking lot in his parents' new VW Golf so he could practice driving with a stick shift for his driver's license test. Of course, you said "Yes" and devoted several afternoons to patiently coaching him on the nuances of achieving precisely the right balance between clutch and accelerator. When the car jerked and stalled, stalled and jerked, you didn't sigh, scream or give any hint of exasperation. All you said was, "Try again," and, after a real sharp jolt, "You'll get it. It takes a little time." Your calm demeanor never wavered even when a series of particularly violent jolts left you wondering if Medicare would pay for several months in traction.

As predicted, he did "get it," got his license and before long was zipping around the streets in his neighborhood and on Long Island parkways much too fast for your taste, but smoothly and lurch free.

When winter rolls around, the two of you go to Austria to ski, and you rent a car with a manual transmission, partly because it's cheaper than an automatic but mainly because you enjoy driving a stick shift once a year. It always takes a few minutes of adjusting to a strange car and to shifting gears again by hand before you are comfortable. After that you don't think any more about it.

But your traveling companion does. You hear a voice from the passenger's seat, a voice that is unrelenting for a solid week, from rental of the car to its return. It says, "You're in the wrong gear," or "Do you know you're in third?" or "Can't you find reverse yet?" After you have pulled into a fairly steep, icy driveway, you're told you did it all wrong; You shouldn't have been "gunning the motor like that." After two or three of these instant reviews, you touch his knee and say, "I've done this a time or two before, you know." He nods, but since he drives a stick shift all the time and you don't, he feels entitled to offer daily critiques.

He has also decided that, since it's just the two of you, this would be a good time to give you some buddy-to-buddy investment tips. He doesn't understand why you and Grandma have your savings invested in various funds in a bank. "I wouldn't let other people be in control of my money," this Warren Buffet in the making says. I try to explain that there are experienced professionals handling our funds and that historically the stock market has always generated higher returns than other forms of investment. He thinks corporations, all of them are out to screw him, me, you and that tree over there, and he repeats, "I just wouldn't let other people be in control of my money."

We're on a ski vacation, a time when all you should worry about is the snow, your skis, your boots, how you're making or not making your turns, whether you're planting your poles too late to get a silky ride down the mountain and how wonderful that first beer of the day is going to taste. Because of all that, you nod and change the subject, maybe ask about that one run right after lunch when he whizzed ahead of you, and it took you ten to fifteen minutes to catch up. You decide against making a joke, something along the lines of whether he would feel better if you and Grandma got a bigger mattress and saved large pickle jars, giving us two safer places to stash our cash.

Also left unsaid is that two of those big bastard corporations somehow contributed money for the old geezer's retirement, and because of them he can afford to pay for meals, lift tickets, lodging, beers and, oh yes, that rental car. In a few years I'm hoping Irene and I can revisit with our first grandchild, Nicholas, the subject of where we keep our money and have a good laugh about it over a beer. After several hugs, we'll then ask how his job is at that God awful, blood-sucking company where he's about to be promoted into Management.

The Good News: *His views on the evils of capitalism don't sound all that different from the ones expressed by his grandfather half a century ago.*

Having A Good Time Silently

When you see an older couple in a restaurant not saying much to each other, don't assume they are bored and not enjoying themselves. They may be having a great time merely watching and listening to everything going on around them. Irene and I do this all the time.

One summer Sunday we decided to go to a museum on Long Island about an hour from us and stop along the way for lunch. Not knowing the area all that well, we weren't sure where we would end up eating. A couple of miles from the museum we passed an interesting looking clam bar, but, seeing no place to park, we drove on. Shortly afterward we saw the museum and kitty-cornered from it a restaurant with lots of cars in a big parking lot. It looked like a place where you go for special occasions, not for an ordinary Sunday lunch. It was fancier than we had in mind, and we looked at each other, then pulled in, and briefly discussed if we were dressed properly. I was wearing shorts, a baseball hat, a T-shirt and an unbuttoned dress shirt. We decided what the hell; if they don't like the way we look they'll tell us to leave.

The host didn't bat an eye. Although the restaurant was packed with what we were told was a high school graduation party, he took us immediately to a table about five feet from a piano player in a tuxedo. After Irene suggested that might be a bit noisy, the host led us to a table right next to the bar. It was the only table in the bar area and faced a fireplace decorated with flowers. In fact everywhere we looked there were flowers, including painted flowers on the ceiling above the fireplace. "It looks like a funeral home," I said, and Irene agreed.

The host took our drink orders, iced teas, after naming seven or eight alcohol and sugar-fired drinks they served for Sunday lunch. The teas were enormous, the size of Super Gulps at 7-Eleven. We soon discovered we were sitting near the flight path to the rest rooms. A parade of women went by, usually two or three at a time. One lady in black made two quick trips. She was wearing sandals with black strings that you wind around your legs up to about mid-calf. As she was returning from the second trip, I told Irene, "It's not every day you get to see Victor Mature."

While I was taking a census of the ladies on their way to and from the restroom, Irene was noticing there was no one eating, at least not any one in our line of sight. "How late is the museum open?" she asked. I held up five fingers. We had three hours before it closed.

Our appetizers eventually arrived and were delicious. We sat for quite a while before we were told, "Your meals will be right out." In this part of Long Island "right out" is slang for 30 to 40 minutes. As we waited, Irene began to fret about a table of four. They had been there when we arrived and still had no food. The man at the table was making his way through a glass of red wine, and if he was perturbed you couldn't tell it by looking at the back of his head, which I was. The grandmother among the four was playing a game of some sort with a girl of about eight. I thought perhaps they were going over the invitation list for the girl's wedding 16 years off.

Young people, who probably were somewhere between 17 and 22 years old, kept walking by the bar area to go outside and then returning, after a smoke I would guess. A few of them would go up to the bar and order a drink for their table before heading out the door. One young man shouted out an order for a margarita, and, as the bartender acknowledged that, walked eye socket first into the edge of the door. He must have had a very sore face the next morning.

Suddenly, Irene got excited. "There's someone chewing," she shouted. Wow. Dish after dish quickly was brought to the tables by the wait staff, though still nothing for the table of four near us. Our entrées appeared—beef ribs for Irene, salad niçoise for me—and we both enjoyed every bite. We agreed to have coffees and share a dessert. Somewhere between these two events food was delivered to the table of four, and Irene immediately felt much better.

Victor Mature wasn't the only actor we saw that day. The host, wearing a black polo shirt and yellow pants, looked like Chazz Palminteri. I was sitting with my back to the bar, ready to hit the floor in case someone stormed in, guns blazing.

While we waited for the check, I went to the men's room and flinched when I saw a tall man with a very red face standing near the urinals. It was a statue, but so real looking I didn't realize it right away. The statue didn't have to go so I cut ahead of him.

The meal was a little on the expensive side for a casual Sunday outing, but the food was good, and Irene and I enjoyed ourselves even though we said very little to each other for the two hours we were there. It doesn't take a hell of a lot to entertain many of us old-timers.

The Good News: *"Victor Mature" didn't follow us across the street to the museum.*

What's With All The Tears?

After a guy turns 65, his tear ducts apparently decide it's time to imitate the rest of the body—to sag and leak. You'll be watching a movie or TV program and discover there are tears in your eyes. For no good reason. It's embarrassing as hell, and you hope no one notices.

One night NBC Nightly News did a story on a surge in births among members of the 82nd Airborne at Fort Bragg, North Carolina, and every time they showed a baby I got all watery. What the hell was that all about? The babies were perfectly healthy. They weren't born with some horrible deformity, didn't have some rare disease, or weren't so early they didn't stand much of a chance to make it. They were beautiful, normal babies, so why was I crying?

Could it be because I realized that the tiniest person in our family, Cristiana Jaclyn McCoy, who was less than two years old, would be our last grandchild, the last little one we would get to scream and clap for as she mastered those very complicated tasks of walking and talking? Was I going to start bawling when she first called me "Gah nah" or the baby-talk equivalent of "that smelly lump with big teeth?"

Nah, I don't think Cristiana was the sole reason. Long before she arrived I noticed I had problems during emotional scenes in movies, especially those involving older fathers and their children. When you're in a dark theater, it's not a major problem, but if you're watching a movie at home with the lights on the manly thing to do is to try to conceal that you're all choked up, that you're nothing but a big cry baby.

Coughing is an acceptable distraction at home, giving

you an excuse to whip out your handkerchief. Another tack that I've used successfully is to suddenly stand up, blurt out, "I'll be right back" and race for the john. Loud farting also works. It's marvelous at diverting attention because it triggers immediate outrage in any and all women in the room and instant, nearly uncontrollable laughter in any male over three years old. (This chasm among the sexes over the acceptability of "pants music" is part of God's grand design, and there's nothing any of us can or should do about it.)

A good friend my age confirms he also tears up more easily these days. He calls it "blubbering." Having already seen a movie doesn't mean you won't blubber when you view certain scenes for a second, third or fourth time. I lose it whenever I watch Richard Jenkins get up at an iron miners meeting in *North Country* to defend his daughter (Charlize Theron) and to denounce his fellow miners for sexually harassing her and other women in the company.

As usual, Irene knows what's happening. Why wouldn't she? If you're at a movie theater and the person next to you has taken off his glasses 17 times in four minutes, isn't that a hint? After a movie, we always sit quietly and watch the credits and that gives me time to dry off all my wet surfaces before heading to the lobby. At home if a movie gets to me, I have real problems locating my voice. I may manage to gasp, "That was really powerful," but the giveaway that I'm on the verge of sobbing is that my voice is 18 octaves higher than normal.

Although this part of aging is a real pain in the ass, I intend to keep watching films and TV programs and no doubt "blubbering." The next time you go to the movies you might want to look around at the old guys there. That fellow four rows from the back with a baseball cap, a hoodie and sunglasses isn't an unspeakable lecher. Just a reasonably nice, older gentleman who pays his bills on time, loves his family, loves his country and cries at the movies. Now stop staring and let him enjoy a good cry, alone.

The Good News: *None of the people you once reduced to tears at work know anything about this side of you.*

In The Waiting Room With Shorty And Stretch

At times you and your wife go to the doctor's office together because one of you has a potentially serious problem and the other goes along for support. Other times you're there together simply because of logistics. One autumn evening Irene had an appointment for a flu shot before we went out to dinner, and I dropped her off and headed to the liquor store. (Do I have my priorities straight or what?)

When I came back, there were two older women waiting for the elevator up to the doctor's office. They appeared to be strangers. The shorter of the two began listing her allergies, and the taller one responded with hers. As we got in the elevator, they both agreed that shots didn't work. They were in such complete agreement about the ineffectiveness of allergy shots that they each said it five times. Never bashful, I offered my opinion: "Shots do work. Whiskey shots." The taller one, Stretch, left the elevator mumbling.

I took a seat in the waiting room next to Irene. Stretch sat next to me and said, "Whiskey shots. I'll have to remember that." After the shorter one, Shorty, finished a conversation at the reception desk, she took a seat next to Stretch and began cataloging the diseases or conditions she has or has had. Stretch tried to match her illness for illness until Shorty mentioned body parts she has had removed.

At some point Shorty moved to the other side of the waiting room and her cell phone went off. Loudly. The theme from "The Sting." Shorty apologized and then announced to all of the 15 or more people in the room that she had been thinking of changing her ringtone, that she's tired of "The Sting." Turning to a 30ish man in the room, she said, "You're too young to know 'The Sting.'"

Guy: "I know 'The Sting.'"

Shorty: (Disbelieving) "How do you know 'The Sting?'"

Guy: "They sell videos."

That hushed Shorty for a spell but then she decided—there in the doctor's waiting room with 15 others—to pick a new ringtone for her cell phone and to audition all the options. One after another. "Oh, I'm sorry that's pretty loud isn't it," she eventually conceded.

Irene missed all the business with the cell phone, having been summoned, mercifully, to get her flu shot before "The Sting" began playing. We were soon out of there and on our way to dinner. When Shorty's turn with the doctor came, I wonder if he treated her for what she came in for or for bruises around the head and shoulders suffered at the hands of waiting room vigilantes.

The Good News: *It's not nice to yell at old folks, so sometimes we do get away with more than we should.*

Toast

"1. To heat and brown (bread, for example) by placing in a toaster or an oven or close to a fire." *The American Heritage Dictionary of The English Language.*

In the old days when Irene and I had jobs, we got out of bed about the same time, but she had to leave the house before I did so she was always a couple of steps ahead of me and we were never in each other's way. Nowadays she's always in the way at breakfast.

My first move in the kitchen is to pour some juice. The second is to reach in a cabinet for my vitamins. Most mornings she is standing right in front of that very cabinet. A fire hydrant. Not about to move or be moved. She could be doing one of several things. Splitting an English muffin. Waiting for a piece of bread or an English muffin already in the toaster to pop up. Slicing a banana. Looking for the holder she can never find for her soft-boiled eggs. Thinking about slicing a banana. Taking her pills. Making a grocery list. Looking out the window at the neighbor's house.

Whatever it is, she is in charge of this space and is not about to budge. Although I did my exercises before coming downstairs, I get in another two or three reps on the arms and legs by reaching around her to open the cabinet door.

I suppose I could move the vitamins to a different location, but I like where they are just fine. It gives me an excuse to keep using one of my favorite morning lines, "Got enough room?" I would miss hearing Irene's standard response, "What do you need?" It tells me another day has begun and that neither one of us is about to change our habits, especially the irritating ones.

I love the lady, like being around her, and am not bothered in the least that she knows much more about most things than I do. But after all these years together I'm still mystified by some of the simple, basic things she doesn't understand despite my repeated attempts to set her straight. We can start with toast. The woman does not know what toast is. Toast comes in one color. Brown. It is not tan. It is not beige. It does not look like saddle soap. Nor is it white bread that is barely warm. Toast is brown. It says so in the dictionary. Why she can't accept the definition provided by scholars baffles me.

She also doesn't comprehend the concept of what a slice is. When we have company and there's dessert—usually served in the living room—those in the know will race to take up a position near the cake or pie before Irene gets there with her knife. If left unchallenged, she will put on your plate a piece of cake big enough to be sublet. Soon cries of, "Whoa! Stop! Who's that piece for?" reverberate around the room. Supersize doesn't come close to describing her slices. To the loudest complainers her usual defense is, "I'm trying to get rid of it." So far she has always said "it" and not "you."

During our meals alone, repetitive questions are a frequent aggravation. We can sit down for dinner at 7:15 with our plates loaded with, let's say, beef roast, potatoes, green beans and carrots, and at 7:22 she will say, "Please have some more green beans." I reply at 7:22:05, "No thanks. They're good but I'm full."

At 7:25 I hear, "Sure you don't want more green beans? I'm going to throw them away if you don't." I love green beans but again, I decline. There will be more chewing and talking, and somewhere around 7:29 will come the accusation, "Well, you won't eat leftovers," which isn't entirely accurate. Leftovers from Monday served on Tuesday?

Absolutely. Leftovers from some unspecified period—perhaps the Reagan administration? Uh-uh. A devotee of soup, Irene often will end up saving the green beans for that but not before one more try. "Sure?" "Sure," I say.

Then there is the Irene at dinner in restaurants where she possesses half the attributes of a good gunfighter: quick hands but slow eyes. We will be seated, given menus and bread and told what the specials are. After a little back-and-forth about what sounds good, she settles on veal Marsala as her entrée. Fine. Once I have made up my mind I put down my menu. Why? Because this is a restaurant not a study hall. Not Irene. She keeps reading the menu. "Just seeing what else they have," she calls it. This is particularly infuriating if I'm really hungry. I will see our waiter a split second after he has turned his back on our table. He figures they obviously aren't ready to order yet because the lady still has the menu in front of her face.

He reappears at some point, takes our order, and I brace myself for Act Two of our little dinner drama. When the food arrives, I hear, "Oh, that sauce looks good." Or "Shoestring potatoes!" followed by, "Let me try one." Ka-bam! Her fork or spoon is in my dish before I have had a bite. "How's my meal?" I ask.

She claims she only does this because she knows it irritates me. It really does. I'm sure I'm just as aggravating. For years I have eaten salad with no dressing on it. Nothing. Nada. It confuses many waiters and bothers Irene. Every couple of weeks she will ask from the kitchen, "Are you sure you don't want some dressing on your salad? It looks so dry."

Dry? Where does she get these crazy ideas? As someone with long experience in the matter, I don't think that cramming leafy spinach, raw broccoli, red onions and chickpeas in your mouth and attempting to swallow it all can be properly classified as "dry." It's a little batty is what it is.

Yet skipping a thick, creamy salad dressing means I'm eating healthy, so it's okay if I have a second drink with dinner. Most people believe salad dressing gives the greens and whatever some flavor. That's true but more importantly it can also hide how rusty and wilted the lettuce under the goo is. After I have a large, goo-less salad, I understand why Elsie the cow is always pictured with her mouth open. She's about to belch from all that grass.

You're supposed to be comfortable in your old age, and it's so comfortable knowing Irene and I aren't going to change our ways. We are going to keep doing the predictable over and over. I wouldn't have it any other way. On almost any evening I will be in the kitchen cleaning up after a good dinner fixed by Irene, and she is the living room reading or watching TV. She will know that before I finish the pans I will holler to her from my position over the kitchen sink, "Are you comfortable?" To which her unwavering reply will be, "Oh, yeah." If I didn't ask and she didn't answer, something would be wrong.

We're also both comfortable with the knowledge that we're slowly shrinking. Neither of us is as tall as we were 10–20 years ago nor do we stand as straight as we once did. I used to tell people I was 5' 11½ ." Now I may be all of 5' 9" at the most. After Irene and I realized we were shriveling, we developed a theory: we may not actually die. We may just get so short you can't see us. Between now and then, if you do see us, please wave.

The Good News: *Not too long ago, we bought a new toaster, and now we have real toast—brown toast—most mornings. If our theory about death is right, one of these days the toast is going to be both bigger and darker than we are. If we're wrong—and in our minds we know we are—we still hope there's a long stretch ahead before "we're toast."*

www.ingramcontent.com/pod-product-compliance
Lightning Source LLC
LaVergne TN
LVHW091224080426
835509LV00009B/1159